About Pfeiffer

Pfeiffer serves the professional development and hands-on resource needs of training and human resource practitioners and gives them products to do their jobs better. We deliver proven ideas and solutions from experts in HR development and HR management, and we offer effective and customizable tools to improve workplace performance. From novice to seasoned professional, Pfeiffer is the source you can trust to make yourself and your organization more successful.

Essential Knowledge Pfeiffer produces insightful, practical, and comprehensive materials on topics that matter the most to training and HR professionals. Our Essential Knowledge resources translate the expertise of seasoned professionals into practical, how-to guidance on critical workplace issues and problems. These resources are supported by case studies, worksheets, and job aids and are frequently supplemented with CD-ROMs, websites, and other means of making the content easier to read, understand, and use.

Essential Tools Pfeiffer's Essential Tools resources save time and expense by offering proven, ready-to-use materials—including exercises, activities, games, instruments, and assessments—for use during a training or team-learning event. These resources are frequently offered in looseleaf or CD-ROM format to facilitate copying and customization of the material.

Pfeiffer also recognizes the remarkable power of new technologies in expanding the reach and effectiveness of training. While e-hype has often created whizbang solutions in search of a problem, we are dedicated to bringing convenience and enhancements to proven training solutions. All our e-tools comply with rigorous functionality standards. The most appropriate technology wrapped around essential content yields the perfect solution for today's on-the-go trainers and human resource professionals.

www.pfeiffer.com

Essential resources for training and HR professionals

About ASTD

ASTD is the world's leading association of workplace learning and performance professionals, forming a world-class community of practice. ASTD's 70,000 members and associates come from more than one hundred countries and thousands of organizations—multinational corporations, medium-sized and small businesses, government, academia, consulting firms, and product and service suppliers.

ASTD marks its beginning in 1944 when the organization held its first annual conference. In recent years, ASTD has widened the industry's focus to connect learning and performance to measurable results, and is a sought-after voice on critical public policy issues.

For more information, visit www.astd.org or call 800.628.8723 (International, 703.683.8100).

About This Book

Why is the topic important?

Reducing the time it takes to get employees up-to-speed has a direct and measurable effect on profits, turnover, and employee morale. The longer it takes employees to become proficient, the longer it takes to reach desired levels of productivity. Delays in reaching proficiency can result in high error rates and lost customers. This issue is of particular importance for organizations involved in major change initiatives where the workforce needs to be prepared to move quickly in a new direction, such as when a company is

- Moving work to a new location—outsourcing
- Experiencing high turnover
- Merging or acquiring businesses
- Downsizing or changing what employees do
- Experiencing health and safety issues
- Changing business strategies
- Moving into new markets

What can the reader achieve with this book?

This book provides the reader with a systematic approach to reducing time to proficiency by mapping and reengineering Learning Paths. In addition, it provides the reader with a practical approach to managing this type of training initiative and demonstrating results. The reader will also gain new insight on how to accelerate the pace of learning while driving down the overall cost of training.

How is this book organized?

This book is organized in three parts. Part I presents the Learning Path Methodology, which is a systematic approach to reducing Time to Proficiency. Part II, Doing the "Right Training," shows how to use the Learning Path Methodology to connect training to business needs and planned changes. Part III, Doing the "Training Right," provides practical methods and techniques for implementing a Learning Path and building training that accelerates Time to Proficiency. The CD that accompanies this book provides the reader with tools and templates for implementing a 30/30 Plan, which is designed to reduce Time to Proficiency by 30 percent in thirty days.

Learning Paths

Increase Profits by Reducing the Time It Takes Employees to Get Up-to-Speed

Steve Rosenbaum • Jim Williams

Linking People,
Learning & Performance

A Wiley Imprint
www.pfeiffer.com

Published by Pfeiffer
An Imprint of Wiley.
989 Market Street, San Francisco, CA 94103-1741   www.pfeiffer.com

1640 King Street Box 1443
Alexandria, VA 22313-2043 USA
Tel 800.628.2783   703.683.8100
Fax 703.683.8103
www.astd.org

ISBN: 0-7879-7444-7

Library of Congress Cataloging-in-Publication Data
Williams, Jim
  Learning paths : increase profits by reducing the time it takes for employees to get up-to-speed / Jim Williams and Steve
Rosenbaum.
      p. cm.
  Includes bibliographical references and index.
  ISBN 0-7879-7444-7 (alk. paper)
  1. Occupational training. I. Rosenbaum, Steven C. II. Title.
  HD5715.W53 2004
  658.3′124—dc22

Acquiring Editor: Matthew Davis
Director of Development: Kathleen Dolan Davies
Developmental Editor: Susan Rachmeler
Editor: Rebecca Taff
Senior Production Editor: Dawn Kilgore
Manufacturing Supervisor: Bill Matherly
Printed in the United States of America
Printing 10 9 8 7 6 5 4 3 2

CONTENTS

Chapter 2: Getting Started 27

Chapter 3: Measuring Time to Proficiency 39

Chapter 4: Mapping Learning Paths 57

Chapter 5: Finding Quick Hits 73

CONTENTS OF THE CD-ROM

Overview

Step 1: Getting Started

30-Day Planning Calendar

30-Day Action Plan

Readiness Assessment

Selecting a Function

Selecting Learning Path Team Members

Learning Path Email Invitation

Step 2: Learning Path Kickoff Meeting Email Invitation

Kickoff Meeting Invitation Email

Kickoff Meeting Agenda

Learning Path Presentation

Learning Path Presentation PowerPoint Presentation

Step 3: Measurement

Measurement Planning Meeting Email Invitation

Measurement Planning Meeting Agenda

Time to Proficiency Baseline Measures

Time to Proficiency New Employee

Time to Proficiency Summary

Measurement Results Meeting Email Invitation

Measurement Results Meeting Agenda

Step 4: Research

Research Meeting Invitation Email

Research Meeting Agenda

Learning Path Research Plan Template

Research Sources Checklist

Research Interview Guide

Questionnaires (Incumbent and Manager)

Step 5: Mapping a Learning Path

Learning Path Mapping Meeting Email Invitation

Learning Path Mapping Meeting Agenda

Learning Path Template

Step 6: Quick Hits

Quick Hits Meeting Email Invitation

Quick Hits Meeting Agenda

Quick Hits Action Plan

Learning Path Template

Step 7: Implementation

Implementation Meeting Email Invitation

Implementation Meeting Agenda

Implementation Action Plan

Step 8: Coaches Training

Coaches Training Email Invitation

A Coaches Training Course Outline

Step 9: 30-Day Presentation

30-Day Report Email Invitation

30-Day Report Meeting Agenda

30-Day Report Template

30-Day Report Template PowerPoint Presentation

Tool Kit

Readiness Assessment

Selecting a Function

Selecting Learning Path Team Members

Time to Proficiency Baseline Measures

Time to Proficiency by New Employee

Time to Proficiency Summary

Learning Path Research Plan

Learning Path Template

Quick Hits Action Plan

Learning Path Evaluation Checklist

Proficiency Planning Process

Learning Path Planning Process

Learning Path Tracking Sheet

Learning Path Project Plan

Self-Study Project Plan

Self-Study Tracking Sheet

Cost Elements

Training Methods Comparison Sheet

Transition Plan

Transition Issues Action Plan

FOREWORD

WHEN I READ THIS BOOK FOR THE FIRST TIME, there were two things that really stood out for me. First, the authors recognize the need to match the speed of developing a workforce to the pace of change. The concept of "Time to Proficiency" as a driving force is a fascinating and needed approach. Second, I was pleased that this book wasn't another untested theory. Instead, it was a detailed system that I could implement with my clients tomorrow.

Having been in the field of human resource development for almost thirty years, I'm often asked what has changed the most since I started. Clearly the pace of business and speed of change, along with the extensive use of technology, are far and away the most significant developments. There is also a growing demand to make everything enterprise-wide and real-time. As someone who has been responsible for human resource development from the inside and as a consultant working with human resource executives and change agents from the outside, I'm always faced with the challenge of not only preparing the workforce to handle change but to get ahead of the curve.

I've known Steve Rosenbaum and Jim Williams professionally for many years. I first met Steve in 1980 when I was the director of human resource development for the Gelco Corporation, which at the time was one of the fastest-growing companies on the NYSE. Later I moved to Wilson Learning Corporation as director of quality consulting and leadership product management, where I started to see the world as an outside consultant, and I worked with Steve on several projects there. When I joined GE as director of human resource development, my first challenge was helping with the integration of four acquired businesses, while simultaneously building the GE culture. Jim Williams was a colleague at GE, where we had similar roles in different business units. I introduced Jim to Steve and I was interested in the work they were doing together.

Today, as the director of training and organizational consulting at Ceridian, I continue to work on projects with Steve and Jim. I was really honored when they asked me to write this foreword because I had witnessed several successful projects using the Learning Path system.

Here's what impresses me the most about the book. First, the book is comprehensive and practical, not theoretical, and the authors have used the methodology successfully with many organizations in a variety of situations. Whatever the business strategy, Learning Paths can make sure people are ready to deliver on it fast, whether it is a new system development and implementation project, a reorganization, outsourcing, new product introduction, or any other change.

Second, I think the measurement piece is critical. At the top of the list for anyone responsible in implementing change is to answer the question, "How do I know when I am there?" Learning Paths is not only a measurement and measurement system but a practical process for how to get there. "Time to Proficiency" is a breakthrough idea and a very practical method to track and account for results. It is also a key component of the Learning Path system, which is to create capability, productivity, and positive results in a hurry, faster than any other method or methodology I've seen.

Third, applications for *Learning Paths* are unlimited. You can use all of it or key segments. It can be used for major complex projects, for getting one critical employee proficient, or for helping him or her get better at doing the job.

Fourth, there is a good blending of strategy and tactics. From what I've seen, there are too many partial approaches to getting a workforce ready to perform at high levels. Many good strategies fall apart during implementation and many of the tactical tools that are out there don't connect to the big picture. *Learning Paths* is a practical tool that does both. One of the key reasons is the authors' background and experience. Jim has the "inside out" perspective. As an internal HRD professional at GE and IBM, he has had to live with his initiatives from concept and implementation to long-term results. Steve brings the objective "outside in" perspective, working on hundreds of successful projects from DuPont to Disney. Jim and Steve, as a team, have produced exciting results in a variety of situations from moving work offshore to major restructuring/organizational change initiatives.

I think you've found a great book here. You'll be pleasantly surprised as you begin to try out the principles and concepts in this book. If you're an HRD professional, it's like being a kid in a candy store.

Ed Robbins, Director of Training and Organizational
Consulting for Ceridian Human Resource Solutions

ACKNOWLEDGMENTS

W E WOULD LIKE TO THANK those who have made contribu-
tions to this book and who have helped us in our development as
learning professionals. First, we would like to thank Al Kennel, Senior Vice
President of Human Resource Management, GE (retired), and Ed Robbins,
Director of Training and Organizational Consulting for Cerdian Human
Resource Solutions, for their extensive and invaluable review of this book.

Thanks to our editors, Matt Davis at Pfeiffer and Mark Morrow at
ASTD, for their early support, and to Maureen Sullivan, editor and publisher
for DBM Publishing, for her advice and coaching, and to Jeanne Cormier,
DBM coach.

We would also like to thank Nick Maras, Vice President of Institutional
Advancement, Century College, for introducing the Learning Paths concepts
into the nation's college system, and thanks to Vinod Khanna, managing
director of Tidesurge Technologies Ltd. (U.K.), for helping us bring the

Learning Path Methodology to international clients of Business Process Reengineering and Outsourcing.

Jim would also like to thank the following people, who provided a lot of support and encouragement over the years. First, a special thanks to Bob Corcoran, GE Chief Learning Officer, for his inspiration and professional guidance and to the GE business leaders in India, including Tiger Tyagarajan and Rajeev Vaid.

Thanks to Pritash Mathur, Master Black Belt, GE India, who helped apply Six Sigma to "Learning Paths" and to the measurement of "Time to Proficiency." Jim would like to thank all those in the Learning Services function at GE India for their outstanding implementation and exciting results. Thanks to those in Hungary for their groundbreaking work in Eastern Europe and thanks to his colleagues in the U.S., including the members of the Advanced Leadership and Facilitation Network at GE, for the chance to work with and learn from a dynamic group of professionals, including Chris Corwin, Mike Markovits, Melodee Morrison, Ellie Murphy, and Randy Ruckdashel.

Jim wants to extend a special thanks to his early mentor, Fred Guth, Education Manager, IBM (retired), who was always interested in "doing the right training and doing the training right," and to his friends and colleagues at IBM, especially Bill Matson, Vice President, HR, IBM. He would also like to thank his wife Debbie, writer and editor extraordinaire, whose fine eye and mind have helped to shape this book, and his children, Carolyn and Paul, who have been a constant source of inspiration and learning. Finally, he would like to thank his parents, Jack and Isabel Williams, and his large, extended family.

Steve would like to thank those individuals we have worked with over the years who have helped shape our thinking about training and development. Thanks to Gloria Stock-Mickelson, Manager, Education & Training, Carlson Wagonlit Travel Associates and Cruise Holidays. Working with Gloria has provided an invaluable opportunity to try new and innovative training strategies.

Steve would also like to thank fellow consultants James Lynn, Ed.D., Lynn & Associates, and Al Frank, Ph.D., Learning Masters, who have really served as mentors over the years. Steve would also like to thank those consultants he has had the pleasure of working with on dozens of projects over the years, including Ira Kasdan, Performance Builders, Karin Johanek, Aspire Consulting, who led a team of writers on the India project, and Donald V. McCain, Ed.D, Performance Advantage Group.

Steve would like to thank his parents, Dave and Joyce Rosenbaum, for their support over the years, including golf lessons when he was growing up. He would also like to thank his uncle, Harry Rosenbaum, who spent a lot time reviewing this book.

Finally, a special thanks to Steve's wife, Pamela Jameson, who played a significant role in editing and reviewing this book while she was publishing her own book, *Unlucky Star: A Novel Based on the Life of Hawaii's Last Princess*. Steve and Pamela would like to thank their dogs, Koa and Lili, who participated on all the conference calls and spoke up very loudly.

THE LEARNING PATHS METHODOLOGY provides a structured approach to increasing business profits by shrinking the time it takes for employees to get up-to-speed. Every day an employee isn't ready to work and ready to be productive costs money and customers, as well as lowering morale and increasing unwanted attrition.

Learning Paths is a practical and measurable approach to accelerating the learning process for new and existing employees as well as future business leaders. It's an in-depth synthesis of our fifty-plus years of combined experience working from both the inside and the outside of America's leading companies. You'll find this book is short on theory and long on practical methods, techniques, strategies, and tactics.

Everything in this book is structured around a specific Learning Path for one individual function or job. Years ago, we used to look at a curriculum, a developmental plan, or just a simple training plan instead of a Learning Path. However, it's unrealistic to think that going through a series of training programs is going to be enough to ensure that what you learn transfers to the job. In fact, you see it all the time where someone leaves training with high marks and then can't replicate what he or she learned back on the job.

Traditionally, it has always been difficult to measure training and link it directly to improved performance on the job. Someone is always willing to claim that the improvement came about because of some other factor. We've found that with a Learning Path approach we can easily measure results and tie them directly to going from one end of the path to another. By doing this, we are able to show real bottom-line returns that are directly attributable to this methodology.

In this book, we will be defining the Learning Path approach, including how to measure it, implement it, and show bottom-line results. While everything in this book is based on working with a wide range of types and sizes of businesses, we've tried to show how Learning Paths can be applied to the functions you will find in most companies. We've loaded the book with examples from call centers, transaction centers, customer service, internal and external sales, and manufacturing. Learning Paths will also work in other business environments and at all levels of an organization. They can be quickly adapted for positions that require certification, licensure, or continuing education.

Another key motivating factor in looking toward Learning Paths as a solution is the constant push to maximize or, better stated, cut training dollars. In the past, we've been able to use the dollar savings generated by Learning Paths to fund other training initiatives.

We feel that, for even the most experienced training professionals and business leaders, these ideas and strategies can easily be adapted and implemented and will yield immediate results.

How the Book Is Organized

As you look at the structure of this book, you will notice it is divided into three parts:

- Part I covers the Learning Path Methodology. In the first eight chapters you go through the major steps and strategies for building Learning Paths.

We show you how to use all of the forms and templates for effectively leading and managing a Learning Paths Initiative. There is also a detailed case study example that illustrates Learning Paths in action.

- Part II is called "Doing the Right Training." This set of chapters goes through the various strategies, methods, and techniques you can use to make sure that the training within a Learning Path is correct, complete. and tied to business needs.

- Part III shows you how to "Do the Training Right." What this means is making sure that the training within a Learning Path is delivered in the most cost-effective manner. We also show how to structure training so that it transfers to the job in a more effective manner.

In the back of the book you will find a section on Frequently Asked Questions. Finally, there is a Tool Kit, which provides blank copies of all of the forms and templates we use in building and implementing Learning Paths.

30/30 Plan CD

This book also comes with a CD that contains everything you will need to implement the 30/30 Plan, which is described in more detail at the end of Chapter 1. In essence, what you will find on the CD are the planning guides, forms, templates, meeting agendas, presentations, and other tools you will need in your first thirty days. One of the early steps in the process requires presenting the concept of Learning Paths to others in your organization. On the CD, you will find a PowerPoint® presentation, complete with a script in the notes pages that you can customize and easily use.

Who Should Read This Book

This book presents a complete methodology for establishing, building, and implementing Learning Paths. It includes both strategies and tactics. As a result, it should provide something new and different for all members of the training and human resources functions.

For those at a more senior level, it provides a method for better aligning the training and development of employees with the goals and strategies of the organization. For those at a management level, it presents a way to organize and implement a learning initiative, including how to manage the initiative and build support with others. At the implementation level, it provides techniques for building or restructuring individual pieces of training.

The book also has a broader appeal to consultants as a way to sell, build, and implement training. As organizations continue to outsource more and more of their training functions, this pool of consultants is rapidly growing. As a result, we feel that there is a significant need for the type of methodology we present here.

Finally, we've tried to write this book in a very practical and accessible manner. You'll find that it is written in almost a narrative manner to give you the impression that we're sitting around a table having a conversation. We've also loaded the book with a lot of tools and templates so that it will be easy for you to try out the concepts. We think that, while a great deal of what you will read is intuitive, the real insight you will gain will be the result of mapping out your first Learning Path.

Key Terms

In this book, we use a number of key terms. They are the language of Learning Paths. The key terms are

30/30 Plan. This is the initial part of the Learning Path Methodology where the Learning Path team goes from the Readiness Assessment through the Quick Hit Process. This activity leads to a 30 percent improvement within the first 30 days. It is designed to build support for expanding a Learning Path Initiative.

Accelerating a Learning Path. This is a process of applying the set of learning principles defined in this book to reengineer a Learning Path.

Directed Self-Study. This means that students are going through a training program with the help and coaching of a manager or supervisor. It can refer to print-based, multimedia, or electronic formats.

Graduation Day. The day formal training ends.

Independence Day. The day proficiency is achieved and the employee is able to perform without constant supervision or assistance.

Independently Productive. Being able to perform a task or function without supervision to a predefined level of proficiency.

Learning Path. Maps the complete sequence of learning activities, practice, and experience required to become independently productive in a function or task.

Learning Path Methodology. The disciplined system for implementing a Learning Path Initiative.

Learning Path Team. A team assembled specifically to build, implement, and maintain a Learning Path for a given function.

Proficiency. Being able to perform a given task or function up to a predetermined standard. Proficiency and independently productive are often used as synonyms.

Proficiency Model. The total set of proficiencies that define a job or function. In this book, it is described as a significant upgrade from a competency model.

Quick Hits. The initial improvements to a Learning Path that happen immediately after mapping one out for the first time.

Time to Proficiency. The time it takes to reach a predetermined level of proficiency. In other words, the time from day one to independently productive.

Part I

The Learning Path Methodology

PART I CONSISTS of eight chapters that present the Learning Path Methodology. Here is a brief summary of what you will be reading about in each chapter.

Chapter 1: From Graduation Day to Independence Day

Chapter 1 presents the rationale for Learning Paths and describes the overall Learning Path methodology as well as the 30/30 Plan. This chapter includes a detailed definition of a Learning Path and the critical concept of Time to Proficiency. You will see why we shift the focus from what it takes to complete the training to whatever it takes to get up-to-speed on the job.

Chapter 2: Getting Started

Chapter 2 begins a series of chapters that walk you through the Learning Path Methodology. In this chapter, you will read about conducting a readiness assessment before you start, selecting a function as a starting point, and assembling a Learning Path Team. At the end of this chapter is a case study that illustrates how to build and implement a Learning Path. This case study is carried through Chapter 6.

Chapter 3: Measuring Time to Proficiency

Chapter 3 explains how to measure a Learning Path. In this chapter, the Learning Path Team establishes Time to Proficiency and uses it as the baseline for future improvement. In this chapter we also discuss ways to set up experiments for determining the effectiveness of training and, finally, how to link Time to Proficiency to business results.

Chapter 4: Mapping Learning Paths

Chapter 4 walks you through the process of collecting the information a Learning Path Team will need. It then shows you how to conduct a Learning Path mapping session. In the case study is a completed *current* Learning Path.

Chapter 5: Finding Quick Hits

Chapter 5 shows you how to find and incorporate changes to a Learning Path within the first thirty days. It is focused on how to capture short-term gains, including the most obvious and needed improvements, into a revised Learning Path. The case study shows a *revised* Learning Path that includes all of the Quick Hits.

Chapter 6: Accelerating Learning Paths

Chapter 6 is really all about reengineering a Learning Path. While the Quick Hits chapter focuses on how to make improvements or revise the path, this chapter looks at building a new Learning Path that better fits with the key principles of accelerating a Learning Path. The case study shows a *final* version of a Learning Path that is very different from the revised Learning Path in the previous chapter.

Chapter 7: Transition and Maintenance

Chapter 7 discusses two key topics. First, how do you make the shift from what's happening now to a new Learning Path? Second, once a Learning Path is in place, how do you keep it current, correct, and complete? This chapter also shows how to report out results from a Learning Path Initiative.

Chapter 8: Managing Learning Path Projects

Chapter 8 provides tools and guidelines for smoothly managing a Learning Path Initiative. It's placed in this part of the book to put closure on the process described in the first seven chapters.

Part I builds the foundation for Learning Paths. Parts II and III go on to provide more strategies, tools, and examples that will add more depth to what you will read in Part I.

1

From Graduation Day to Independence Day

HOW DO YOU GET a large number of employees up-to-speed quickly? The answer to that question has been the focus of our work over the past two decades and has led to the discovery and evolution of the concept of Learning Paths, a different way of looking at training.

Costly Delay

Imagine that you're now in charge of a five-hundred-person call center that largely focuses on customer service. Since this is a very typical call center, you probably have at least 50 percent attrition and you're likely to be expanding and even adding new locations. This means that you will need to be continually hiring and training two hundred to three hundred new employees each and every year.

From Day One until Proficiency, which means when each new employee is fully up-to-speed, there is a high cost of errors and lower productivity and a risk of alienating customers. It's fairly intuitive that it costs more if it takes an extra six months for a new employee to get up-to-speed. However, it's even more apparent when you actually quantify and measure that difference. In this book, we will be showing you how to do this type of measurement and also how to document bottom-line results from Learning Paths.

Today in our typical customer service call center a new class of thirty employees starts every month. They go through a two-day orientation, followed by three weeks of classroom training. Those who successfully make it through training and pass all the tests spend the next thirty days nested or buddying up with a lead or top performer. It's a period of probation with a lot of one-on-one coaching.

If you asked supervisors in the call center how long it takes a new employee to get up-to-speed, they would probably say sixty days. However, that's just the official training period. In our experience, if you actually looked at performance measures you'd find that it can take two to three times longer than the official training period for a new employee to reach the level of an average performer.

Why is there such a large gap between the end of training and reaching the level of an average performer? We've uncovered three major reasons. First, when you have a large block of up-front classroom training, you usually also have a large data dump that is easily forgotten. By the time Week Three rolls around, it's difficult to remember what happened on Day Three. Without direct application to the job in a real, live experience, most of what happened in the classroom will have to be repeated several more times.

Second, most of the time we underestimate the amount of practice it takes to learn a new skill. You can learn the basics of keyboarding in an afternoon, but it takes several weeks of practice to be able to type fifty words per minute. When you look at a more complex skill, such as making a sales presentation, this takes even more practice. In reality what often occurs is that most of this practice happens unsupervised and in front of customers. It's a very expensive way to learn by trail and error. And many bad habits are picked up and passed on this way. The sink-or-swim approach has many hidden costs, where 20 percent make it and 80 percent do not. Think of the efficiencies if we can turn that around so that 80 percent make it and only 20 percent do not.

3 Third, once the classroom training is over, there isn't a lot of consistency or structure for the on-the-job training or coaching. Depending on who you are paired up with in our call center, the type of training you receive will be all over the map. You're even likely to get a coach who says, "Forget about what you learned in class. I'll show you how this is really done."

We've also found that when you actually dig into the formal training and look at what's being taught, you almost always find that a portion of it is out-of-date, no longer applicable, or just plain wrong. Since most training isn't continuously updated and revised, it's often one step behind. This is an issue that we are going to address strongly in this book as we go along.

Imagine now that you're in charge of an outside sales force or a manufacturing plant or even an accounting department. You have exactly the same issues of getting new employees up-to-speed and also existing employees who aren't there yet. You have the same expense of errors and lost business that comes with new employees. The only difference is that in some of the more complex jobs the actual start-up time may be as long as nine months to two years.

Independently Productive

Before we define Learning Paths, it's important to clarify what it means to be up-to-speed. One of the key terms we use is "independently productive." This is the point in time when you are left totally on your own and that you can do your job without asking questions or making mistakes. It's also the time when you feel confident and competent in your job.

In a lot of jobs that operate in a team environment, the concept of "independently productive" is particularly important because the support of the team often masks what individuals are actually contributing.

Think about the jobs and positions you've had in the past. It always took a while to learn the job, but at some point in time, you felt that you had the job mastered. As we set out specific measures for being independently productive, we are going to do so in terms of *proficiency.* Proficiency is when a new employee achieves a predetermined level of performance on a consistent basis. Proficiency can be defined in numbers of transactions, dollars sold, defect rates, customer satisfaction scores, or anything else that is measurable and related to results. If we look at it from the customer's perspective, we might ask how long it will take to completely replace the person who has left.

So with that foundation, when we talk about getting up-to-speed or start-up time, we are going to be doing so in terms of Time to Proficiency. We know that Time to Proficiency has a dollar and cents cost to the business that grows with every extra day, week, or month. We also believe that reducing Time to Proficiency is the most significant contribution the training function can deliver to the organization.

The concept of a Learning Path is based on our belief and experience about how people actually learn. Before we describe the methodology of Learning Paths, take a look at this example and description of how people learn.

How People Really Learn

Underlying every concept and principle in this book is our firmly held belief about *how people really learn.* While much of this is very intuitive, because it's how we've all learned what we know and can do, in most organizations it seldom shows up in how training is delivered. We'll be referring to this as *the difference between a curriculum approach and a Learning Path.*

The easiest way to look at what we are talking about is through a couple of brief examples. Learning how to play golf is a great example because it requires a wide range of skills and knowledge, from analytical thinking to psychomotor skills. As we go along, we are going to contrast learning to play golf with learning how to sell.

Using the traditional method of training, let's break golf down into its component parts and structure classroom training for each. For our new golfers our three-week training program looks like Exhibit 1.1.

Exhibit 1.1. Three-Week Golf Training Program

Week 1	Week 2	Week 3
• Introduction to Golf • The Basics: Grip, Stance, and Ball Position • The Full Swing	• Chipping and Pitching • Putting	• Course Management • Specialty Shots • Tournament Play

This is very intensive training. With hard work, you might even be able to break 100 by the end of the third week. But getting to a top performer level, which means shooting in the 70s, is likely to take months or years to learn, not three weeks. The same holds true for selling. New salespeople come out of their three-week to six-week training with the basics but are usually six to nine months away from being even average performers.

So what's missing? The major difference between someone who shoots as low as the 90s and an A-level player shooting in the 70s is about 85,000 practice balls. When you consider that a large bucket of balls at a driving range has 85 balls, this will add up to about 1,000 large buckets or around one large bucket a day, every day for about three years. An elite player, either a top amateur or a tour-level player, will hit four to five million practice balls in his or her lifetime.

A few other things are missing also. There's a big difference between playing five to ten rounds of golf a year and playing seventy-five to one hundred rounds of golf annually. This also doesn't include playing in tournaments and matches. There's a lot of difference between playing with friends and playing in front of thousands of people for money.

So let's go back and look at our three-week golf curriculum. Where is all the practice and experience? It's not there. Now let's switch over to a typical sales curriculum. Consider how many sales calls it takes before you really know how to sell. Depending on the complexity of the sale, it's probably in the hundreds. And it also involves a wide range of sales situations and challenges to achieve some level of mastery. However, you'll seldom if ever see that detail assessed and documented.

One work environment that starts to address this issue can be found in call centers. Typically, call center training starts with one to six weeks of classroom training, followed by some type of on-the-job coaching. This is usually a highly unstructured period of time—up to ninety days—where you'd work with a supervisor or top performer. While this is a step in the right direction, it's still a slow and ineffective way to learn and also falls months short of the usual six months to get up-to-speed.

Here's what really happens. We're going to assume that the training is well-built and instructionally sound. When you go through weeks of classroom or formal training, you are bombarded with all sorts of information, techniques, processes, and expert presentations. By the time you get to Week Three, you no longer remember much of what you did in Week One.

The situation gets even worse by Week Six. As you step out into the job for the first time, you're still a long way from being an average performer. What's missing is all those practice balls, or a few hundred sales calls. You have a big investment in all these new employees now, but your break-even point is still a long way away.

The major shift in the way training needs to be structured involves integrating formal training, practice, and experience along a Learning Path, and not in a topic-by-topic curriculum. In our golf analogy, learning how to putt might have the Learning Path shown in Exhibit 1.2.

As you can see, there is a lot of time spent in structured practice, which in our sales examples is all the joint calls, ride-alongs, and practice presentations. While this often happens informally, it's not as valuable or powerful as when it is integrated back into the first few weeks on the job with a great deal of structure, rigor, measurements, and feedback.

If golf or sales isn't your game, here are a couple of other examples to illustrate the point about how people really learn. Have you ever mastered playing a video game or wondered how someone got so good at playing PAC Man®?

Exhibit 1.2. Putting Learning Path

Day	What	How
1	**Putting Basics**	• 30 minutes lecture/demonstration • 60 minutes practice putting with a coach
	Short Putting (1 to 10 Feet)	• 30 minutes lecture/demonstration • 120 minutes short putting drills with a coach
2	**Long Putting (10 to 50 feet)**	• 30 minutes lecture/demonstration • 120 minutes long putting drills with a coach
	Reading Greens	• 30 minutes lecture/demonstration • 120 minutes reading greens drills with a coach
3-5	**Practice Putting**	• 500 short putts (150 uphill, 150 downhill, 200 side hill) • 500 long putts (150 uphill, 150 downhill, 200 side hill) • 3 putting tournaments

It's simple. If you spend about twenty or thirty hours playing the game, it starts to get easy. You quickly stop thinking about how the game works and start to actually play the game. Soon you will begin to see patterns and methods for how to beat the game. You plow through the frustrations and failures in the first few hours to quickly master the game. The PAC Man class might have shortened your learning time, but it can never substitute for the hours of practice.

Part of this came strongly into focus for us a few years back while working with an apprenticeship program with the State of Minnesota. They had nicely set out what was very similar to a Learning Path in order to achieve an apprenticeship certificate. They were working mostly with manufacturing jobs. What you would see was a formal training program followed by the number of hours working on a specific machine. You'd see a one-week classroom program of working on a small printing press, followed by 2,000 hours of on-the-job experience. There might be four or five pieces of equipment followed by job experience ranging from 2,000 to 5,000 hours. It's not just practice, but people you have met, things you have done, places you have visited, tests, people you have coached and taught, other jobs you have done. All of these can go on a Learning Path.

So the question arises, if it takes 2,000 hours to learn how to run a small printing press, how many hours does it take to make a high-level, complex sales call? You'd probably have a tough time finding that number in any sales training you've ever seen.

In connecting training to how people really learn, you need to focus not just on what they need to learn but also on the practice and experience they will need to achieve a high level of performance. It's moving away from topic-by-topic curriculums to Learning Paths.

Learning Path Methodology

We are going to define a Learning Path as *the chronological series of activities, events, and experiences that goes from Day One to Proficiency.* Our goal is to accelerate the Learning Path to reduce Time to Proficiency.

At a very high level, there are six steps in the Learning Path Methodology, as shown in Figure 1.1.

Step 1: Select a Function

The starting point is always to select a function, task, or process to work with. The first function is usually a revenue-generating function with direct customer contact. It's also a function that has an executive level sponsor or champion who will give full support.

Step 2: Determine Time to Proficiency

Time to Proficiency is the baseline measure for this initiative. All results will be measured against this amount of time. This step requires defining proficiency and then establishing a true measure of Time to Proficiency.

Figure 1.1. Learning Path Methodology

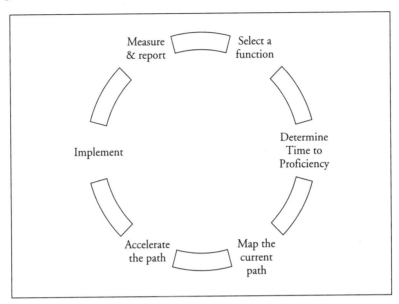

Step 3: Map Out the Current Path

This is a process of documenting everything that currently happens from Day One to Proficiency. It's not the outline of the current training program. It needs to include all of the other practice and experience that new employees currently go through. However, it's likely that you will have to build a consensus about a current path because you will find a lot of gaps and differences in how current employees actually learned their jobs.

Step 4: Accelerate the Learning Path

There are a lot of ways to accelerate a Learning Path, including using technology. In most cases, accelerating a Learning Path involves going to a more effective learning model and then rearranging or reengineering the path to fit that model.

This is also an opportunity to look at changes in the job, the business, or future strategies to make sure that the training fits both current and future needs.

Step 5: Implement the Path

Once a revised Learning Path is in place, the next step is to implement the path. This means making a smooth transition from the old path to the new one. In addition, it also includes putting in place a maintenance plan to make sure the path is always current and correct.

Step 6: Measure and Report

The final step involves measuring Time to Proficiency as it is reduced and then reporting results to management. This level of measurement and reporting gains support for building Learning Paths for other functions and continuing the initiative.

The 30/30 Plan

When we actually work on Learning Paths, we don't go through the entire process in a single pass. Instead, we use the first thirty days to generate some significant and early results to build support and momentum. We call this first pass the 30/30 Plan. This means we will be identifying ways to reduce the current Learning Path by 30 percent in the first thirty days. What this means is that there will be a new Learning Path in place that is 30 percent shorter and is ready to implement.

The big difference between the full model and the 30/30 Plan (as shown in Figure 1.2) is a change in Step 4, Accelerate the Learning Path. At this point, we will be looking for what we call "Quick Hits" instead. What tends to happen when you map out a Learning Path for the first time is that there are obvious improvements that can be made or Quick Hits.

The biggest gain always comes from the fact that you put new employees through a structured path that continued once up-front training stopped. For example, we did some work with a large company that had branch offices in all fifty states. Typically, there was some up-front training for new assistant branch managers. However, they picked up most of their training from others in the office when time was available. They learned how to enter a new

Figure 1.2. 30/30 Plan

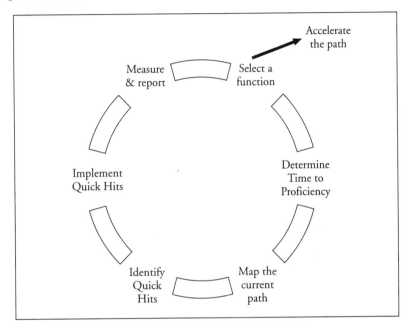

order by watching someone else take an order. This is your basic over-the-shoulder training method.

What the formal Learning Path did was identify everything a new assistant branch manager needed to know how to do and plot it all on a time line. We also organized it in a way that sequenced how the job can be learned the quickest. We revised existing training materials so that they could be used as self-study just prior to a manager showing how to do a task. For example, the student would read about doing a cash transaction immediately before being shown how to do one. The reading material then served as a reference guide.

When we measured the length of time it took to develop a new assistant manager, we found it was reduced from anywhere from twelve to eighteen months to around six months. In many respects, what we did was remove most of the waiting time.

The second place you will often find immediate gains comes from eliminating the need to have a full class before you start training. When we've worked with larger sales forces we see this situation all the time. The practice is to hire salespeople and then have them come to the home office for three weeks of training when there are enough new hires to warrant a class. Filling that time until the first class was a lot of paperwork, riding around on calls, and reading through a lot of product literature. This waiting time could take anywhere from three to six weeks.

The change that was made was to create a Learning Path that structured the waiting time so that it created extensive prework for the classroom training. As a result, all new employees entered the classroom training with a similar level of knowledge and experience and then the classroom training was more focused on practice and application. We were able to reduce the classroom time by a full week. In addition, sales managers stated that the salespeople were much better prepared to make calls once they left training.

The third and perhaps most obvious place to reduce the Learning Path is to cut out everything that isn't necessary. We did some international work where new employees needed to have a basic background in American history and culture. After looking at what was being taught, it was very obvious that there were a number of wasted days spent covering information that most Americans wouldn't know or care about.

In another instance, we worked with an insurance company in their transaction processing and found that two of the processes being taught in the training actually no longer existed. Those elements were removed and training was quickly reduced by a day or two.

These are just a few examples of many. If you take the time to lay out a Learning Path for any function, you will easily see immediate gains. Most will be very obvious. The 30/30 Plan gets you through the first version of your Learning Path and will provide you with the results needed to make the case for continuing to upgrade and revise the Learning Path.

Now let's look at the first thirty days. This plan starts once you've selected a function to work on and scheduled a kickoff meeting with the team that will be working on this function. It's critical to pick a function with a business or functional leader who will be

- A champion for the Learning Path
- Committed to the methodology
- Convinced about its value
- Respected by most senior leadership
- A thought leader respected by peers and juniors

A sample project plan is shown in Exhibit 1.3.

Exhibit 1.3. Sample 30/30 Project Plan

Day	Actions
1	• Hold a kickoff meeting 　- Define proficiency 　- Develop measurement plan 　- Develop research plan
2 - 7	• Gather measurement data • Conduct research
8	• Map out current Learning Path
9 - 10	• Brainstorm Quick Hits
11 - 13	• Revise and validate current Learning Path
14 - 27	• Build additional materials such as job aids and reference guides (These may take longer but they are added as they are ready)
27 - 29	• Conduct training for coaches
30	• Replace current training plans with the Learning Path

At the end of the first thirty days, you will most likely need to make a report of what you've been able to accomplish. Figures 1.3 through 1.5 are quick examples of that type of report.

Figure 1.3 is a quick recap of what you've accomplished to date. It's good to remind everyone that you've really accomplished a lot.

Figure 1.4 presents the definition of proficiency that will serve as the basic line for all future measures.

Figure 1.5 is a quick recap of the measurement to date. The first column shows that the existing training program lasts three weeks. When surveyed, everyone thought that it takes six weeks to become proficient. That was after an initial three-week probationary period. When time to proficiency was actually measured, it turned out to be ten weeks. The new Learning Path, which will start with the next group of new employees, is structured to last seven weeks. That 30 percent reduction was created by applying all the Quick Hits, including adding more on-the-job coaching.

Figure 1.3. 30-Day Results

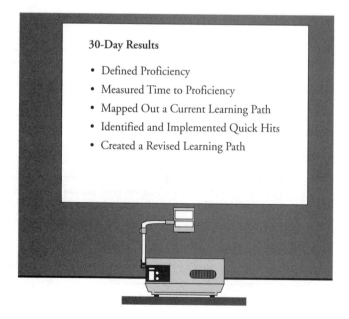

Figure 1.4. Definition of Proficiency

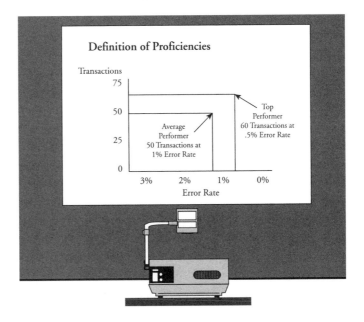

Figure 1.5 Time to Proficiency

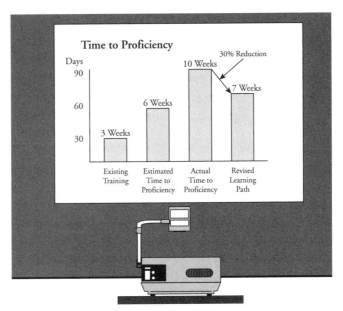

Summary

In this chapter, we defined Learning Paths and set out the overall Learning Path Methodology. We also contrasted Learning Paths with a traditional training curriculum and presented the difference between Graduation Day and Independence Day. The critical takeaways from this chapter include:

- Every day an employee is not fully up-to-speed costs the organization money in terms of lost productivity, increased errors, and often lost customers.

- Proficiency is a result of more than just formal training. It also requires extensive practice, experience, and on-the-job coaching. That's why there is a significant difference between Graduation Day and Independence Day.

- Most organizations vastly underestimate the time it takes for employees to reach proficiency. When time to proficiency is first measured it quickly becomes apparent that there are significant opportunities for improvement.

At the end of the chapter, we introduced the 30/30 Plan, a quick-start version of the Learning Path Methodology that is designed to reduce a Learning Path by 30 percent within thirty days. The 30/30 Plan is expanded and reinforced on the CD that comes with this book.

Now that we've given you a big-picture look at the Learning Path Methodology, we are going to go into the details of each step in the process of building Learning Paths.

2

Getting Started

IN THIS CHAPTER, WE are going to be looking at how to get off to a fast and productive start. We will also be looking at putting in a solid foundation that will help you avoid potential problems down the road. As you get started, there are four key things that you will need to do.

1. Conduct a Readiness Assessment

2. Select a Function

3. Assemble a Learning Path Team

4. Hold a Kickoff Meeting

Readiness Assessment

The purpose of a Readiness Assessment is to help you make sure you have adequate support up-front and that you can begin to identify any obstacles or barriers as you get started. Exhibit 2.1 is a quick Readiness Assessment you can use.

There is always a lot of skepticism and foot dragging in any initiative that involves change. As we have stated, the 30/30 Plan is one strategy you can use to overcome some of these initial hurdles. Anything that you can do to show results early will make this or any project go much more smoothly.

Selecting a Function

The next step after an assessment is to pick a function. While we believe that every job should have a Learning Path, a logical priority is to start with revenue generating jobs, jobs that are closest to the customer and employees who are newest with the company. Think of how often your customers encounter people who are the newest with the company, lowest paid, and least well trained. Training can help offset the other two.

In your first attempts to measure and work on Learning Paths, it's important to select functions or processes that will have a significant impact on the business and provide the most useful measurement data. Since working on Learning Paths is a different approach, there will be a lot of skepticism. Therefore, being able to show quick results as well as long-term financial benefits will be the key to keeping the momentum up. There's always a lot of push back on change, so you will need all the ammunition you can get to support your efforts.

Start by creating a short list of the functions or processes that have the largest numbers of employees. Then identify those that are revenue-generating and/or have high customer contact. Some of the functions that you might want to consider include:

- Order Taking
- Transaction Processing
- Customer Service

Exhibit 2.1. Readiness Assessment

Directions: *Rate each question from 1 to 5. (1 = Low and 5 = High) For any item rated as a 1, 2, or 3, write in a required action to address each issue.*

Questions	Rating	Required Actions
1. How important is reducing Time to Proficiency to your top management?	1 2 3 4 5	
2. How willing are your business leaders to be champions or sponsors for a Learning Path Initiative?	1 2 3 4 5	
3. How willing is the organization to commit the time of required individuals to actively participate on a Learning Path Team?	1 2 3 4 5	
4. How well do you understand the concepts and principles of the Learning Path Methodology?	1 2 3 4 5	
5. How well does your organization create and accept change?	1 2 3 4 5	
6. How willing are your current training staff, vendors, and consultants to participate in a Learning Path Initiative?	1 2 3 4 5	
7. What is the level of your organization's capabilities to conduct training research?	1 2 3 4 5	
8. What is the level of your organization's instructional design capabilities?	1 2 3 4 5	
9. What is the level of your organization's project management capabilities, including presentations and report writing?	1 2 3 4 5	
10. How willing are managers to coach and develop their people?	1 2 3 4 5	
11. How willing is the organization to commit financial resources if and when training needs to be updated, created, or revised?	1 2 3 4 5	
12. How well is formal on-the-job or self-study training accepted by the workforce?	1 2 3 4 5	
13. How willing is the workforce to share and discuss information about how they do their jobs?	1 2 3 4 5	
14. How experienced is your organization in measuring training and/or quality?	1 2 3 4 5	
15. How ready do you feel your organization is to begin a Learning Path Initiative?	1 2 3 4 5	

- Accounts Receivable

- Assembly

- Outside Sales

- Telemarketing

Put off looking at management functions until a later round of Learning Path development. You will also be able to demonstrate a greater benefit by selecting functions where the number of employees is rapidly expanding and where there are some significant quality and turnover issues. Remember, everything is going to work better if you can get a big success early. These types of functions will also be the easiest to measure and, in fact, many of the measures will already be in place.

The template in Exhibit 2.2 will help you identify and evaluate functions that will be the best starting point. It's important to overweight the factor of support from a sponsor or champion.

Exhibit 2.2. Selecting a Function

Function	# of Employees	Projected Growth	Management Support	Priority	Other Factors
Sales	42	10%	High	2	Fall Product Launch
Customer Service	120	25%	Moderate	1	High Turnover

Learning Path Teams

Once you have selected a function, you are ready to assemble a Learning Path Team. These are teams that consist of key stakeholders for your selected function. Stakeholders are defined as anyone or any group that is affected by the work done by the targeted job or function. The team can certainly be working on multiple functions, if they are related. You work with a team for three key reasons. First, the team provides expertise and insight that you won't come up with on your own. Second, there's a lot of work to be done and why not get others to help.

Third, you're going to need the support of these people to make any changes work. This team needs to feel that they own this Learning Path and that it's their idea, not yours. Consider setting up new teams with one or two people who have successfully mapped and accelerated other Learning Paths.

The planning guide in Exhibit 2.3 will help you identify members of your Learning Path Team.

Exhibit 2.3. Selecting Learning Path Teams

Role	Description	Team Member
1. Executive Sponsor or Champion	- Ensure that resources and time are allocated to this initiative - Address any organizational issues or barriers	
2. Project Leader	- Conduct team meetings - Manage the logistics and communications of the initiative - Train team members in the Learning Path Methodology	
3. Subject-Matter Expert	- Ensure that the content covered in the Learning Path is current and complete - Ensure that the research is accurate and complete	
4. Training Leader	- Make sure that the training resources are available and funded to implement this initiative	
5. Instructional Designer	- Ensure that any changes to the Learning Path are instructionally sound - Provide insight into how to improve the Learning Path	
6. Quality Leader	- Provide expertise in measuring training and business results	
7. Other Stakeholders	- Provide experience and validation on how selected functions are performed and measured	

Holding a Kickoff Meeting

In your first meeting with your Learning Path Team, you will be planning out your next thirty days and ending up with a revised Learning Path for the selected function. To help you with this meeting, you can use the Kickoff Meeting Agenda in Exhibit 2.4.

Exhibit 2.4. Kickoff Meeting Agenda

Function:	Location:		
Date:	Time:		
Leader:	Attendees:		
Purpose: To launch the 30/30 Plan and to clarify team roles and responsibilities.			
Prework: Read chapters 1 to 6 of the Learning Path book.			

What	How	Who	Time
1. Welcome members of the Learning Path Team, including team member introductions.	Welcome Activity	Leader	15 min.
2. Give the Learning Path presentation. *(From the 30/30 Plan CD.)*	Presentation and Discussion	Leader	25 min.
3. Provide an overview of the next 30 days and lead a discussion about roles and responsibilities.	Presentation and Discussion	Leader	25 min.
4. Discuss the upcoming measurement meeting; include the materials and information team members should bring to that meeting.	Discussion	Leader	15 min.
5. Set time and date for next meeting and review the 30-day calendar.	Discussion	Leader	5 min.

CASE STUDY: PART 1

Throughout the next several chapters we will be using a case to illustrate how to build, measure, and accelerate a Learning Path. In this case study, we will be using the Learning Path templates to illustrate how they are used.

We are going to call our fictitious company Generic International, Inc. (GII). GII manufactures, sells, and services a moderately technical generic product to businesses in ten countries. They have a five-hundred-person customer service call center that handles inquiries and problem resolution related to the product. Billing issues and order entry are handled by separate functions.

GII has a new employee class of thirty customer service reps (CSRs) that starts every other month. This keeps them about even with the company's growth rate and 40 percent turnover rate. As you look around GII, everything seems to be very typical and, yes, generic.

During a meeting of the executive team, GII's Chief Learning Officer introduced the Learning Path Methodology and led the team through the Readiness Assessment, Selecting a Function, and Selecting Learning Path Team Members. Exhibit 2.5 is the output of their work.

Exhibit 2.5. Readiness Assessment for GII

Directions: *Rate each question from 1 to 5. (1 = Low and 5 = High) For any item rated as a 1, 2, or 3, write in a required action to address each issue.*

Questions	Rating	Required Actions
1. How important is reducing Time to Proficiency to your top management?	1 2 3 ④ 5	
2. How willing are your business leaders to be champions or sponsors for a Learning Path Initiative?	1 2 3 ④ 5	Customer service manager is eager to do this initiative, others are more skeptical. Customer service should go first.
3. How willing is the organization to commit the time of required individuals to actively participate on a Learning Path Team?	1 2 3 ④ 5	
4. How well do you understand the concepts and principles of the Learning Path Methodology?	1 2 3 4 ⑤	
5. How well does your organization create and accept change?	1 2 3 ④ 5	
6. How willing is your current training staff, vendors, and consultants to participate in a Learning Path Initiative?	1 2 ③ 4 5	Trainers don't see a reason to change what they think works now. Try to find an active role for them so they will take ownership.
7. What is the level of your organization's capabilities to conduct training research?	1 2 3 ④ 5	
8. What is the level of your organization's instructional design capabilities?	1 2 3 ④ 5	
9. What is the level of your organization's project management capabilities, including presentations and report writing?	1 2 ③ 4 5	Projects tend to take too long. Trainers are currently going through a project management course.
10. How willing are managers to coach and develop their people?	1 2 3 ④ 5	This is really unknown because the customer service managers are not doing this now.
11. How willing is the organization to commit financial resources if and when training needs to be updated, created, or revised?	1 2 ③ 4 5	Budgets are tight. Will need to show quick results to fully fund this initiative. Proving this approach with one function is mandatory.
12. How well is formal on-the-job or self-study training accepted by the workforce?	1 2 3 4 ⑤	
13. How willing is the workforce to share and discuss information about how they do their jobs?	1 2 3 4 ⑤	
14. How experienced is your organization in measuring training and/or quality?	1 2 ③ 4 5	We will be using Learning Paths to begin to upgrade this capability. May need help from the quality organization.
15. How ready do you feel your organization is to begin a Learning Path Initiative?	1 2 3 ④ 5	

Exhibit 2.6. Selecting a Function for GII

Function	# of Employees	Projected Growth	Management Support	Priority	Other Factors
Customer Service	500	10%	High	1	Need to reduce high turnover.
Sales	75	15%	High	3	Sales force is being reorganized. Training needs to be reviewed when reorganization is completed.
Assembly	300	1%	Moderate	2	They are currently involved with a new quality initiative that is taking all their resources.
Engineering	25	0%	Low	4	They feel that engineers are already proficient when they are hired.

Exhibit 2.7. Selecting Learning Path Teams for GII

Role	Description	Team Member
1. Executive Sponsor or Champion	- Ensure that resources and time are allocated to this initiative - Address any organizational issues or barriers	Jim McMillian, Vice President of Marketing
2. Project Leader	- Conduct team meetings - Manage the logistics and communications of the initiative - Train team members in the Learning Path Methodology	Tom Thomas, Training Manager
3. Subject-Matter Expert	- Ensure that the context covered in the Learning Path is current and complete - Ensure that the research is accurate and complete	Alice Johnson, Customer Service Supervisor
4. Training Leader	- Making sure that the training resources are available and funded to implement this initiative.	Karen Fields, Chief Learning Officer
5. Instructional Designer	- Ensure that any changes to the Learning Path are instructionally sound - Provide insight into how to improve the Learning Path	Kathy Bateman, Freelancer
6. Quality Leader	- Provide expertise in measuring training, designing experiments, statistical analysis, and business results	Al Jones, Quality Control Manager
7. Other Stakeholders	- Provide experience and validation on how selected functions are performed and measured	Bob Smith and Sue Franklin, Top Customer Service Reps (CSRs)

Summary

In this chapter we presented the first few steps that launch the Learning Path Methodology. These included:

- Assessing your organization's readiness to embark on a Learning Path Initiative. Some of the issues raised in this assessment can be dealt with up-front, while others will tend to go away as you produce measurable results in the first thirty days.

- Selecting your initial function as the pilot for Learning Paths. As we've stated, it's critical that this function have a strong and well-respected champion who can pave the way.

- Assembling a Learning Path Team that has the expertise and skills to build a Learning Path as well as any new training that is required.

- Holding your first kickoff meeting.

In the next chapter, you will read about the first major activity for your Learning Path Team. You will learn how to measure Time to Proficiency, which will become the baseline for improvement.

3

Measuring Time to Proficiency

MEASUREMENT IN TRAINING has always been a difficult and controversial issue. How do you attribute success or improvement to a single training event? For starters, it's difficult to isolate the effects of training from everything else that's happening in the business. If you went to a two-day sales seminar and sales went up in the next month, did the training make the difference or did a big customer decide to increase orders for their own reasons?

With Learning Paths we look at measurement from a different point of view. While we always want to make sure that each individual training event is doing its job, we are more interested in the degree to which we can shorten the Learning Path in terms of Time to Proficiency. In taking this approach, we have found that we can apply a measurement rigor that proves the business case for a Learning Path Initiative.

In this chapter, we are going to examine three aspects of the measurement puzzle. First, we are going to show you how to establish a baseline measure for a Learning Path. In other words, what is the current Time to Proficiency with the training that is in place today? As changes are made to the Learning Path, we can determine how those modifications affect the overall timeline.

Second, we are going to look at putting measures on individual learning activities to determine their effect on Time to Proficiency. In particular, we are going to examine how putting hard numbers on the amount of practice and on-the-job experience can reduce the amount of time between Graduation and Independence Day.

Third, we are going to look at how changes in Time to Proficiency can be directly linked to other business measures. For example, if new salespeople begin making sales in week six instead of week twelve, those additional sales can be attributed to the change in Time to Proficiency.

Finding Independence Day

Establishing a baseline really means finding the current Independence Day. What we are looking for is the average time it takes employees to go from Day One to Independently Productive. This will hold true for both new employees getting up-to-speed in a new job or current employees who are on the path from average to top performers. However, in this chapter, we are going to focus on new employees to illustrate the measurement process.

The first step is to define proficiency or what results will be produced when an employee becomes independently productive. For new employees, we often set this benchmark at reaching the level of an average performer. The starting point should be to examine the current performance measures being used and then to establish the level of performance for average and high performers.

For example, reservation agents in a travel center or field sales agents can be used to show the level and types of information that need to be gathered. These examples also illustrate how to create a template that your Learning Path Team can use. For example, reservation agents in a travel center might have measures such as those in Exhibit 3.1 and field sales agents might have measures as shown in Exhibit 3.2.

In both of these functions, you might also have customer satisfaction scores or performance evaluation scores, such as call monitoring scores from the call center. What you are looking for are the most meaningful measures and those that are consistently used by management. There are also a great number of books written on performance management that can help you arrive at objective measurements for almost any function, including management positions and professions such as accountants and engineers.

The next step is to determine the average amount of time it takes to reach the desired level of proficiency. For example, when does a new reservation agent consistently handle twenty calls per day with a call monitoring score of four out of five? One way to accomplish this is to look at the historical performance data for current employees as they went through their initial training. Your ability to do this will depend on the quality of the data you already have. First, we'll examine what to do if you have good data and then look at some alternatives if the data is incomplete or sketchy.

Exhibit 3.1. Reservation Baseline

Time to Proficiency Baseline Measures

Function: Reservation Agents

Performance Measure	How It's Measured	Average Performance	High Performance
Calls per hour	Captured by reservation system	20	30
Reservations per hour	Captured by reservation system	3	5
Average dollar amount per reservation	Captured by reservation system	$1,500	$2,200
Cancellation rate	Monthly sales reports	3%	<1%

Exhibit 3.2.

Time to Proficiency Baseline Measures

Function: <u>Field Sales</u>

Performance Measure	How It's Measured	Average Performance	High Performance
Calls per day	Daily sales reports	3	5
Average sales	Order recap sheet	$10,000	$18,000
Return rates	Monthly sales recap	5%	3%
Number of new customers	Monthly sales report	1 per month	3 per month

We use the template in Exhibit 3.3 to record baseline data for past new employees. It works best if you complete a new template for each new class of employees. For example, if ten salespeople were hired and went through training together, that would be one class. In the template, you want to enter the employee name and date of hire. Next enter the number of classroom days and the number of days of formal on-the-job coaching. Together this will give you Graduation Day. In the final column, record the date the employee reached the level of an average performer.

If you go back and can find data for the last two or three classes, you can summarize that data using the template in Exhibit 3.4.

Keep in mind that by definition we are considering everything that is happening between Day One and Independence Day as the Learning Path. Therefore, days to proficiency is an accurate measure of the length of a Learning Path. If we were to chart this example, it would look like Figure 3.1.

Exhibit 3.3. Time to Proficiency by New Employees

Function: <u>Field Sales</u>

Employee	Date of Hire	Classroom Days	Coaching Days	Days to Proficiency
Bob Allison	1/15	15	20	80
Alice Bodine	1/15	15	20	65
Fred Johnson	1/15	15	20	120
Total/Average		15	20	73

As you can see from the figure, there is a significant time between Graduation and Independence Day. We often refer to this as the "mystery period" because all of the learning that happens during this time is seldom written down and almost always varies from employee to employee. As we go through the Quick Hit process, the largest gains tend to come from reducing the mystery period.

Exhibit 3.4. Time to Proficiency Summary

Function: <u>Field Sales</u>

Number of Employees by Class	Classroom Days	Coaching Days	Days to Proficiency
10	15	20	73
8	15	20	82
12	15	20	85
Average	15	20	80

Figure 3.1. Sales Learning Path

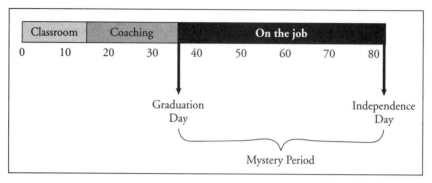

In the absence of historical data, you can use survey data to establish a baseline. However, a word of caution: survey data about Time to Proficiency is almost always overly optimistic. Therefore, it will be important to put in real measures as you go forward. To get the best survey results, you will need to survey both incumbents and their immediate supervisors. Exhibit 3.5 is an example of a survey you can use for incumbents. You can modify it for managers by rewording the questions to refer to their employees instead.

Exhibit 3.5. Time to Proficiency Survey

1. How long was the formal training you received when you started this job?

2. What type of training did you receive after this formal training and how long did it last?

3. Was there a probationary period? How long did it last?

4. How long did it take for you to be able to do this job without supervision?

5. When did you feel confident that you could do this job?

6. How is your performance measured?

7. When did you receive your first average or better performance review?

8. Is there anything you still don't know how to do?

Ongoing Measurement

We've now established a baseline as a starting point. The ultimate measure is always going to be the change in Time to Proficiency. However, as we go forward we want to increase the measurement rigor so that we can more accurately determine the effects of any changes on the length of a Learning Path. We are also going to have a goal of reducing the time spent in the mystery period where everyone is learning on his or her own.

Ideally, we would like to measure proficiency as it changes in each of the key proficiency measures. For example, if we measured calls handled per day for a reservation agent it might look like Figure 3.2.

As you overlay the other proficiency measures, you may find that some are achieved in a few days, while others take weeks (Figure 3.3). This will help you determine which area to focus on to get the greatest gains. For example, if handling calls according to procedure happens in week one, but the number of reservations taken is low for the first thirty days before it spikes up, more attention can be placed on the actual reservations process.

Figure 3.2. Calls Per Day

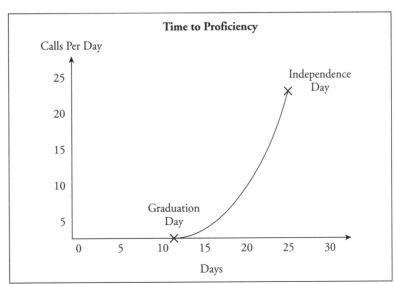

Figure 3.3. Comparing Proficiency Measures

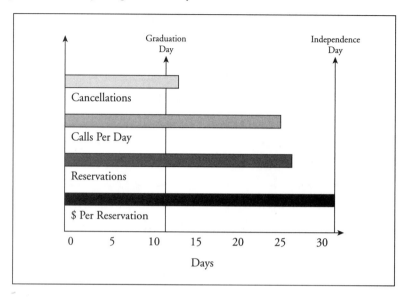

Another way to look at what happens is to get deeper into the actual calls themselves. Let's look at what happens when you plot the Time to Proficiency for the four major types of calls in the reservation agent example, seen in Figure 3.4. You can see that learning how to book an "air only" reservation happens rather quickly. In fact, it happens almost immediately after the reservation agent leaves the classroom training. However, learning how to book cruises and escorted tours takes a lot longer.

As you work through and analyze the data, you begin to find the areas that will have the greatest impact on reducing Time to Proficiency. It would seem in the reservation example that focusing on maximizing revenues from tour and cruise callers takes the longest to learn and therefore may have the greatest effect on Time to Proficiency.

Let's dig into this analysis one level deeper. One of the things that is happening during the mystery period is that employees are getting the practice and repetitions they need to master new skills and learn how to use them in

Figure 3.4. Comparing Call Types

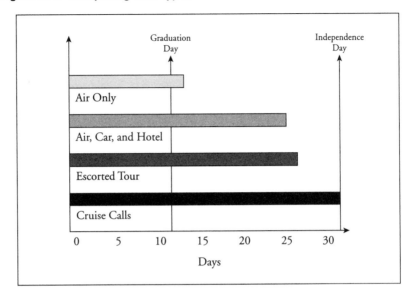

combination. When you are able to identify and quantify this activity, you can then build it into a Learning Path so that it happens sooner. In the reservations example, we could look at what happens to the proficiency level of each call by the number of times it's practiced. The chart would look something like Figure 3.5.

In the figure, we see that it takes about eighty calls to really become good at escorted tour calls. In the Learning Path, we need to make sure the reservation agent gets those repetitions in a structured manner early in the learning, rather than waiting for them to happen. This may mean increasing simulated calls, if we are doing the training during the off-season for escorted tour calls.

As you can see, there are several different ways to look at measuring Time to Proficiency that will help you determine how to structure, formalize, and shorten a Learning Path. It also allows you to set up measurement experiments to see the impact of any changes you make. For example, if you move

Figure 3.5. Comparing Call Types

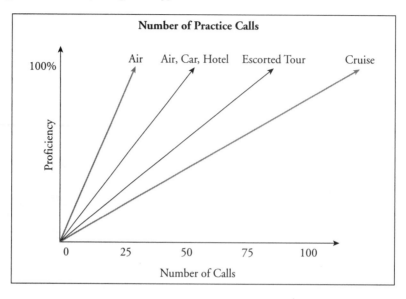

a classroom session to e-learning you can see whether it increased or decreased the Time to Proficiency. If Time to Proficiency doesn't go down, it may mean that there is something that was in the classroom session that did not translate to the e-learning or that it may require more coaching to replace some of the interaction with the facilitator from the classroom session. In any case it allows you to do some concrete analysis with real data.

One of the reasons for adding someone from your quality organization to the Learning Path Team is to add the measurement rigor, such as a Six-Sigma process, to this part of working on Learning Paths. They can also help you determine whether any variation in the data is statistically significant or just noise in the system.

So far we've talked about establishing a baseline and then putting in place the ongoing measurement that will help you identify ways to reduce Time to Proficiency. As you work with the Quick Hit and acceleration processes, allow the measurement to be the check on your success. This will ensure that you are actually improving things rather than just changing them.

Business Results

At the end of the day, your Learning Path Initiative will be judged on what it added to the bottom line of your organization. As we have said, the overriding metric used with Learning Paths is the number of days it takes to reach proficiency. Taking sixty days out of a Learning Path for one hundred employees equals 6,000 extra days of productivity. If this were a transaction processing function, where each employee did fifty transactions, that could mean up to 300,000 additional transactions.

To calculate and report the results of any function, you should start by measuring what an average day of productivity is worth. That would include how many sales are made, how many parts are produced, and how many calls were taken. These are the fundamental measures of production and productivity that probably already exist.

Intuitively, almost everyone sees and immediately agrees that, if a new employee can be productive in forty-five days rather than sixty days, this will have a bottom-line benefit. For someone in sales, documenting the gain can be as simple as adding up the extra sales from days 45 through 60. In Exhibit 3.6, we are going to assume that the desired level of proficiency is $1,000 a day. In each group there are ten new salespeople. Group 1 is on the old Learning Path and Group 2 is on the revised Learning Path.

Exhibit 3.6. Sales Results

Days	Group 1	Group 2
1 - 30	0	0
31 - 45	0	$75,000
46 - 60	$75,000	$150,000
61 - 90	$150,000	$150,000
Total	**$225,000**	**$375,000**

In this example, you can see a ramping up of sales as each group becomes proficient. In this example we are assuming that both groups end up in the same spot. However, in reality Group 2 probably continues to be ahead on the way to higher levels of proficiency. This can be tracked as you gather the actual numbers. In this quick example there is a measurable $150,000 difference.

In a manufacturing environment, you could measure the difference in defect rates or production per hour as each group learns. In a processing center, you could look at the number of transactions or even transaction time. Again, as you measure one group against the other, you have the benefits of extra weeks of activity as well as the benefits of a jump start in the learning process.

An effect that is really important but harder to quantify is the effect of allowing untrained or partially trained employees to deal with customers. It doesn't take many lost customers or lost orders to make a huge financial difference.

Another way to look at the cost and impact of Time to Proficiency is to look at it in terms of a break-even date, which is actually further out than a Time to Proficiency date. (See Figure 3.6.)

Figure 3.6. Finding Break-Even

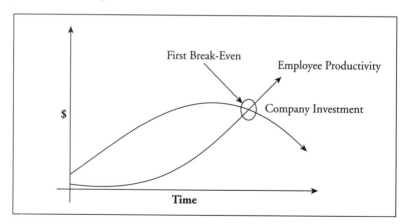

Figure 3.6 shows that the business makes an investment in each new employee in terms of hiring, training, and wage costs. The new employee starts to pay back this cost as he or she becomes productive. At some point, the gain from the employee equals the amount that has been invested. That's the break-even point. For example, if it takes $20,000 to hire and train a new salesperson, how many sales will it take to pay back that investment? Obviously, if you move the Time to Proficiency from eighteen weeks back to six weeks, you're going to reach that break-even point much faster. We've found that this is an excellent chart to help justify working on Learning Paths.

Finally, this approach to linking Time to Proficiency to business results does not preclude other measures of training effectiveness. However, the better the training is, the more likely it will be that the Learning Path will be shorter. This is even true if the actual formal training is longer. If an extra day in the classroom means that employees will be proficient three days faster, it may be a good tradeoff.

CASE STUDY: PART 2

Now let's go back to our case study example. In this part of the case study, the GII Learning Path Team established a baseline measure of ninety-five days to proficiency. Let's look at how they arrived at that date. As we do this, we will be introducing three templates that can be used to record proficiency data.

In the GII call center, CSR performance is measured as shown in Exhibit 3.7.

Supervisors monitor calls throughout the day. They have a ten-point checklist that includes interpersonal and phone skills as well as technical knowledge and following the problem-solving process.

Time to Proficiency was determined by looking at the scores and ratings of the last three new-hire classes. They used two templates, Exhibits 3.7 and 3.8. Exhibit 3.8 captures data for each class by individual. Exhibit 3.9 shows how the information from all three classes was rolled into a summary report.

All ninety new employees went through fifteen days of classroom training followed by thirty days of nesting with an experienced CSR. The research also looked at the total range of days it took to get up-to-speed. As you can see, some CSRs were up-to-speed very quickly, while others took almost an extra month. The averages of all employees in a class and the total average of all ninety employees are shown in the last column. From this the team established a baseline of ninety-five days.

There was a lot of discussion about the wide range in Days to Proficiency and that this was something they wanted to focus on during this process. They wanted to learn more about why some people were getting through quickly while others were not. They also recognized that there was about a forty-five-day gap from the time the nesting was over to when employees reached proficiency. The team recognized that they needed to determine what was happening during this additional time and make sure those events happened earlier in the training.

Exhibit 3.7. Performance Measures

Time to Proficiency Baseline Measures

Performance Measure	How It's Measured	Average Performance	High Performance
Calls per hour	Captured by call system	25 calls	35 calls
Average handle time	Captured by call system	3.45 minutes	3.15 minutes
Completeness of documentation	Review by auditing	98%	99%
Call monitoring score	Conducted by supervisors daily	3.5 out of 5	4.5 out of 5
Problem resolution	Complaint log	85% without escalating	95% without escalating

Exhibit 3.8. Time to Proficiency by New Employee

Customer Service Class 1

Employee	Date of Hire	Classroom Days	Coaching Days	Days to Proficiency
1. Bob Allison	1/30	15	30	91
2. Sue Arlen	1/27	15	30	85
3. Pamela Boyce	1/23	15	30	103
4. Mary Barringer	1/30	15	30	90
5. John Cook	1/30	15	30	78
6. Jim Cronberg	1/27	15	30	110
7. Dale Douglas	1/30	15	30	108
8. Chris Everson	1/30	15	30	87
9. Lynn Feinstein	1/30	15	30	82
10. Linda Grace	1/23	15	30	125
11. Alice Harrington	1/30	15	30	101
12. Fred Hart	1/27	15	30	95
13. Denise Ingersol	1/30	15	30	92
14. Erin Ireland	1/30	15	30	100
15. Kevin Kline	1/18	15	30	88
16. Bob Jones	1/30	15	30	83
17. Martin Marks	1/30	15	30	95
18. Jennifer Ness	1/30	15	30	49
19. Kate Olsen	1/25	15	30	86
20. Mary Olsen	1/30	15	30	98
21. Polly Page	1/30	15	30	101
22. Keith Pollander	1/28	15	30	93
23. Steve Richards	1/30	15	30	104
24. Carolyn Rollins	1/30	15	30	91
25. Betty Stricker	1/30	15	30	42
26. Connie Stringer	1/26	15	30	95
27. Anne Tillis	1/30	15	30	155
28. Terri Thomas	1/21	15	30	79
29. Jim Wells	1/15	15	30	71
30. Sally Wellington	1/30	15	30	87
Total/Average		15	30	92

Exhibit 3.9. Time to Proficiency Measures

Number of Employees by Class	Classroom Days	Coaching Days	Days to Proficiency
Class 1: 30	21 Days	30 Days	92 Days
Class 2: 30	21 Days	30 Days	95 Days
Class 3: 30	21 Days	30 Days	98 Days
Total/Average	**21 Days**	**30 Days**	**95 Days**

Summary

The starting point for working on reducing Time to Proficiency is to establish a baseline. In some environments where there is a lot of performance data, such as in a call center or with a sales force, this will be rather easy. However, this will be more challenging where measurement is highly subjective or where there are no established measurements at all. Also, it's important to try to use real measures rather than surveys to arrive at a Time to Proficiency measure because the survey data is almost always overly optimistic.

A quality improvement specialist can help determine measurements, design experiments, and use statistical analysis to validate that changes in the Learning Path have actually reduced Time to Proficiency.

When you do your first measurement, you should find that there is a gap between the end of any formal training process and achieving proficiency. As you map out a Learning Path, it's critical to try to identify what's happening during that time period so that it can be addressed as you revise the current Learning Path. All too often what's happening in that time period is trial-and-error learning as well as additional practice. If this time period is better organized and structured, you should be able to reduce it significantly.

In the next chapter, you will read about mapping out a current Learning Path. With Time to Proficiency measures, you now have a current end date to the Learning Path, which probably is different than the date training ends. As you do your research for the Learning Path, you will be accounting for this additional time.

4

Mapping Learning Paths

IN THIS CHAPTER, we are going to take you through mapping out your first Learning Path. Even though you will see obvious improvements that can be made as you go along, just jot them down for now and save them until we discuss Quick Hits. At this point, we are simply going to document what currently happens from Day One to Independently Productive. We want to look at not only what happens in the classroom but also what happens on the job. Some of this will be written down and documented well, but a lot of it will be very informal and is often done in different ways at different times by different trainers, managers, and supervisors.

During the mapping process, you will begin to see a lot of variations. That is one major reason why one employee learns quickly and another employee never seems to learn. One employee will have a supervisor who provides a lot of coaching and one-on-one instruction, while other employees will be left to learn on their own. We are going to get a lot of our gains by standardizing what happens according to what works the best.

In addition, the greatest area for improvement is what happens in the mystery period after all the formal training and coaching happen and yet the employee is still not proficient. (See Figure 4.1.) This time period can be weeks, months, and even years, depending on the complexity of the job. Three key questions that need to be asked are:

1. What did you learn after you left training?

2. How did you learn it?

3. Could you have learned it earlier?

Once the Learning Path is mapped, everyone is directed to follow the map until it is upgraded and revised. It's a lot like any process improvement project. Until you have an agreed-on process and everyone uses it, you can't make any significant improvements.

Figure 4.1. Uncovering the Mystery

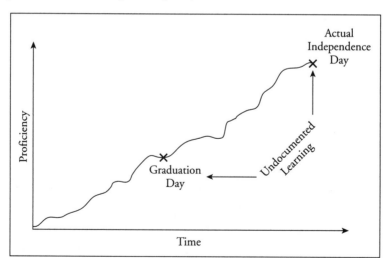

Research

It won't take long, but the Learning Path Team needs to start by doing some quality research. While individual research tasks can be assigned to specific team members by their expertise, team members need to become familiar with their targeted function and its key processes as well as any current training materials.

A good first step is to watch people work. This might include sitting side by side in a call or transaction center, going on sales calls, riding on a forklift, or even visiting a branch operation. Our term for this is *job shadowing*. When you are job shadowing, you are a passive observer trying to understand what happens during a typical day.

At this point, you will also want to start gathering materials and documents. You will use some of this now and rely on a lot of it later, when you start reworking the training. You'll find some of the information you need in big binders, while some of it might be on Post-it® Notes on the wall of a cube. Make sure you collect and look through at least the materials listed in Exhibit 4.1.

Exhibit 4.1. Research Checklist

	Policy and procedure manuals
	Job aids
	PowerPoint presentations
	Charts and graphs posted on walls
	Reports
	Training manuals
	Job descriptions
	Publications
	Websites
	Audio and videotapes
	Computer screen shots

You'll find that a lot of jobs require using specific computer applications and software. It's very helpful to ask the person you are job shadowing to give you printouts as he or she goes from screen to screen. Write your notes about what's happening directly on the printouts.

With all this information in hand, let's go talk to the trainers. Here's where you need to have someone walk you through the current training process. If, for example, there is formal classroom training for the first three weeks, ask the trainer to take an hour or so and walk you through the training. Become familiar with the major topics being taught and the sequence of topics. Later on, when you start working on accelerating the Learning Path, you may even want to sit through the training.

You also want to gather from the trainers all the evaluations, testing and monitoring forms, reports, and other information. Be sure to look for multiple versions of these documents. This will indicate multiple Learning Paths.

Our next stop on our research trip is to talk with managers and incumbents. At this level, we want to talk with managers who are direct supervisors. For incumbents we want to talk with a mix of top performers and average performers who have been in the job two years or less. Some sample interview questionnaires for each group are presented in Exhibits 4.2 and 4.3.

Preparation

You are just about ready to hold a mapping session with your Learning Path Team. To prepare for this session, it's important that you prepare a quick summary of your research to share with the team. You will find a lot of consensus about how new employees learn their jobs. You are also going to find that there are a lot of differences among direct supervisors, as well as a lot of new and good ideas about addressing challenges and improving the training.

In your initial report that will kick off the team meeting, try to take a neutral stance and just report on what you found. Consultants refer to this as a Findings Report. Divide this report into three parts. Part I describes the typical way new employees are trained. Part II describes the differences, depending on direct supervisors and when employees went through training. Part III describes the challenges and opportunities for improvement from the interviewees.

Exhibit 4.2. Incumbent Questionnaire

1. What formal training did you receive? When did you go through that training?

2. What type of on-the-job training did you receive after training?

3. Did you have any type of probationary period?

4. Is there anything in your background before you started this job that helped you learn the job more quickly?

5. What else helped you learn this job? *(Specific experiences, job aides, or mentoring)*

6. What were the most significant obstacles or barriers that you had to overcome while learning this job?

7. What would you do to improve the training or make it easier to learn this job?

Exhibit 4.3. Manager Questionnaire

1. What formal training do new employees receive?

2. How has the training changed or evolved in the past year?

3. What type of on-the-job training, coaching, or mentoring do new employees receive?

4. Who does the on-the-job training, coaching, or mentoring, and what type of training do they get?

5. Is the on-the-job training standardized or does it vary from manager to manager?

6. What were the most significant obstacles or barriers to learning this job?

7. What would you do to improve the training or make it easier to learn this job?

Let's talk for a minute about why you would want to go through this level of analysis and report rather than letting the team work with the raw data. In our experience, you can waste a lot of time in team meetings discussing the obvious and the already known. About 80 percent of your report will be common knowledge. There will also be about 20 percent of the report that is new and it may even be surprising. However, the report advances the starting point by giving the team something to react to instead of just holding an open-ended brainstorming meeting.

Here's a typical example of how this works. If you assembled a team of sales managers and asked them to come up with a list of sales competencies, most of what you will get are all of the known and obvious line items. You'll always see Prospecting, Product Knowledge, Closing, Handling Objections, and Sales Presentation. However, you get a lot more detailed and meaningful answers if you present a model of the typical sales competencies and then ask the team to expand and describe in detail those that apply. Delete or rename any that don't fit. If you want to take this a step further, you could add a rough draft of a Learning Path to your research report.

Mapping Session

In reality, it's probably going to take two or three sessions to get a current Learning Path in good workable condition. You'll also want to allow enough time for everyone to really think critically about the Learning Path so that it is complete and accurate. If you shortcut the time spent up-front, you will probably end up with a Learning Path that looks a lot like the table of contents from the formal training sessions.

Exhibit 4.4 is a quick look at an agenda for a mapping session.

Now for the details. As with any new team, you need to go through the basic set-up of introductions and ground rules. The next step is to provide an explanation of Learning Paths and the process that you will be using. It wouldn't be a bad idea to ask everyone to read this book prior to that first meeting.

Exhibit 4.4. Mapping Session Agenda

Function:	Location:
Date:	Time:
Leader:	Attendees:

Purpose: To map out a current Learning Path.

Prework: Bring all of the research information that you have collected since our last meeting. Read Chapter 4 of the Learning Path book.

What	How	Who	Time
1. Fill in the Learning Path Template with the current training program if one exists.	Team Activity	All	20 min.
2. Discuss and add any training that happens outside the formal training or on-the-job. When there are multiple approaches, discuss and try to select the one the team thinks will be the most effective.	Team Activity	All	20 min.
3. Identify any practice activities or field experience that happens between the end of training and the time employees become proficient.	Brainstorming and Discussion	All	15 min.
4. Discuss how the current Learning Path can now be validated. Who needs to review it in order to make sure that it reflects what's happening now?	Discussion	All	15 min.
5. Set time and date for next meeting.	Discussion and Decision Making	All	5 min.

Present your research report as a discussion document. Reinforce that this report reflects what you found and not your personal opinions. If team members disagree with anything in the report, it will tend to highlight variations in what's happening that you will want to reconcile in this process. Don't get defensive.

In mapping out the path, you are going to be looking at what's happening, when is it happening, and how it is delivered. For example, new employees spend the first two days in new-hire orientation delivered in a classroom setting. Before going into a lot of detail, it's probably a good idea to build a high-level timeline that shows the major blocks of what's happening. A high-level timeline might look like Exhibit 4.5.

The length of this timeline needs to reflect what happens from Day One to your Independently Productive date. You may have a lot of weeks at the end of this timeline where the new employee is just doing the job but isn't proficient yet. Don't make up something to fill in the space if nothing is really happening.

This high-level timeline will be an excellent communications tool when you need to talk with people outside the team. As you change and revise the Learning Path, you also want to revise this timeline. Later on, you will be able to contrast this longer timeline with your newer, shorter timeline.

The format we like to use for a Learning Path is a simple checklist. When the path is built, you will be able to use this checklist to monitor an individual employee's progress through the learning process. Later on, we'll talk about how to dump this checklist into a Learning Management System (LMS). Exhibit 4.6 is a blank template for a Learning Path.

Exhibit 4.5. High-Level Timeline

Week 1	Week 2	Week 3	Week 4	Week 5
New-Hire Orientation	Product Training	Practice and Simulations	On-the-Job Coaching	On-the-Job Coaching
Computer Training	Process Training	Final Exam		

Exhibit 4.6. Learning Path Template

Day	What	How	Materials	Done
	Training Event Description	Training Method Used	Print, Video and Electronic Support	Used Later as a Checklist

1. Enter Formal Training

Start the mapping process by filling in all of the formal training. You want to make sure you fill in all of the major topics, activities, and tests. In the "How" column, you should enter in the method used to teach each topic. These will include: Lectures, Discussions, Role Plays, Games, Tests, Simulations, Field Trips, Reading Assignments, Videotapes, e-Learning, and so forth. The column marked "Materials" is used so that you can easily cross-reference any line item to existing courseware, manuals, or other reference guides. Usually for classroom materials there will be leader's guides, workbooks, and overheads. Exhibit 4.7 is an example of how part of a one-day training session is entered into a Learning Path. Exhibit 4.8 gives an example from a manufacturing plant.

Exhibit 4.7. Learning Path Example 1

Day	What	How	Materials	Done
9	Handling Objections (**4 Hours**) – Handling Objections Process – Common Objections and Answers – Putting It All Together	Lecture Brainstorming Role Plays	Leader's Guide Workbook Overheads	

One of the questions that often arises when mapping out a Learning Path is how much detail to put into each line item. Putting in a line or two about several days of classroom training isn't going to be enough if the Learning Path Team isn't thoroughly acquainted with that program. What we like to do is to create a backup document for all of the major pieces of training that provides the essential details. In Chapter 15 on directed self-study, we've provide a format for a training outline that you can use to record information for each line item of your Learning Path.

Exhibit 4.8. Learning Path Example 2

Day	What	How	Materials	Done
4	Safety Equipment (**2 Hours**) – Footwear – Gloves – Hard Hat – Harness	Video and Discussion	Videotape Workbook Leader Notes	

2. Enter On-the-Job Activities

Next, enter any structured, on-the-job activities, for example, a nesting or mentoring period in a call center. In other functions it might include working on a specific piece of equipment, taking a set number of calls, or completing a project. If it involves a task that is repeated many times, try to estimate the number of times this task is done, for example, make twenty-five sales calls, assemble one hundred circuits, inspect thirty trucks, or reload ink four times. Exhibits 4.9, 4.10, and 4.11 are some examples of entering this type of training into the Learning Path.

Exhibit 4.9. Learning Path Example 3

Day	What	How	Materials	Done
26	Call Practice – Take 25 incoming calls – Evaluate and discuss calls with supervisor	On the Job	Call Evaluation Checklist	

Exhibit 4.10. Learning Path Example 4

Day	What	How	Materials	Done
30	Joint Calls (Observation Only) – Visit 2 existing customers – Make 3 cold calls	On the Job	None	

Exhibit 4.11. Learning Path Example 5

Day	What	How	Materials	Done
30	Collections Calls – Make 5 collections calls – Evaluate and discuss calls with supervisor	On the Job	None	

You'll notice that, as you start to plug in this type of training, you will have a lot of days of the same activity, which is okay. However, you'll find that most of these days are highly unstructured. This will become an opportunity for improvement.

3. Enter Testing and Evaluation

Next, enter any testing and evaluation that is done. If there is none or if it is sporadic, this will also provide an opportunity for improvement. You need to know that employees are moving down the path in a rapid and positive manner. This is something that we will want to address when we look for Quick Hits.

4. Enter Job Experience

As you look at the path you are going to have a lot of empty space. At this point, just enter in "Job Experience." This endless expanse is a gold mine for improvement. But hold off taking action just yet; we want to write down what's happening now before we go to the next step.

5. Reconcile Differences

Finally, you need to reconcile differences. If there are multiple versions of the path or it's different every time a new employee is hired, it needs to be standardized. It's difficult enough to improve one path, let alone many for the same job. Remind the team that what you choose now will most likely change a lot in the next few months but that you need a starting point. Direct the team to select the path that seems to be the most complete and rigorous.

Don't spend a lot of time arguing about which method or path is best. It's going to change quickly anyway. Take a vote and pick one. Then save the other ideas for discussion as you look at Quick Hits and Accelerating the Path. This version is just a stake in the ground.

6. Evaluate

After you've taken your best shot at a current Learning Path, double-check it to make sure it's more than just a training agenda or a series of classroom courses, like a curriculum. Make sure you've accounted for the time out of class up to your Independently Productive date. As a result of this activity, you're going to have a big list of ideas for improvement.

CASE STUDY: PART 3

The GII Learning Path Team spent about a week conducting research before sitting down to map out a current Learning Path. Exhibits 4.12 and 4.13 show the team's Research Plan and Learning Path.

Exhibit 4.12. Case Study Research Plan

Function: Customer Service   Today's Date: 10/20   Estimated Completion Date: 10/27

Research Activities	Action Steps (Who, What, Where, and How)	Conducted By	When
Interviews	Identify and interview the following individuals: – 5 top leads and supervisors – 5 graduates of recent new hire training who have reached proficiency – 10 top CSRs – Customer service center manager	Karen	10/20 - 10/27
Focus Groups	Identify and invite customers for a half-day focus group.	Tom	10/25
Job Shadow	Observe 5 top performers and 5 recent graduates of new-hire training.	Kathy	10/23 - 10/24
Gather Materials	Collect all current training materials and prepare a walkthrough of the material for the team on 10/30.	Kathy and Karen	10/25 - 10/30

Exhibit 4.13. Case Study Learning Path

Current Learning Path

Function: _____CSR_____   *Date:* __2/02/03__

Day	What	How	Materials	Done
1	New employee orientation - Welcome - Company history, goals, and mission - Product overview - Competition - Work rules - HR paperwork - Benefits - Customer service and your role	Classroom	Leader's Guide Workbook Overheads New Employee Orientation Manual HR Benefits Package	
2	Department Presentations - Sales - Marketing - Finance - Production - Engineering - Customer Service - Distribution	Classroom	Overheads Handouts	
3	Visits - Plant tour - Warehouse tour - Customer service center	Field Trip	None	
4	CSE (Customer Service Excellence-Software Program) - Log On/Log Off - Finding a customer record - Change of information - Practice	Classroom	Leader's Guide Workbook Overheads	
5	CSE (Continued) - Setting up a new customer - Checking on order status - Adding journal entries - Sending emails - Practice	Classroom	Leader's Guide Workbook Overheads	
6	CSE (Continued) - Taking a new order - Checking billing status - Practice	Classroom	Leader's Guide Workbook Overheads	

Day	What	How	Materials	Done

7	CSE (Continued)
	  – Sending promotional material
	  – Doing price quotes
	  – Scheduling a new order
	  – Practice
		Classroom	Leader's Guide
			Workbook
			Overheads	

8	CSE (Continued) – Review and practice	Classroom	Leader's Guide Workbook Overheads	

9	Product Presentations
	  – GII - Galaxy
	  – GII - Neptune
	  – GII - Saturn
	  – GII - Jupiter
		Classroom	Overheads
			Handouts	

10	Customer Service Skills
	  – Taking new orders
	  – Handling problems and complaints
	  – Role play and practice
		Classroom	Leader's Guide
			Workbook
			Overheads	

11	Using the Phone System
	  – Features
	  – Logging in and out
	  – Call transfers
	  – Three-way calling
	  – Conferring
	  – Practice
	  – Telephone etiquette
		Classroom	Leader's Guide
			Workbook
			Overheads	

12	Communication Skills
	  – Listening
	  – Business writing
	  – Interpersonal styles
		Classroom	Leader's Guide
			Workbook
			Overheads	

13	Team Building	Classroom	Leader's Guide Workbook Overheads	

14	Call Handling Practice
	  – Listening
	  – Business writing
		Classroom	Leader's Guide
			Workbook
			Overheads	

15-30	Nesting
	  – Working next to a top performer and a lead agent
	  – Listening and taking calls
	  – Receiving feedback
	  – Daily call monitoring
	  – Weekly performance evaluation
		On the Job	Call Observation
			Checklist
			Performance
			Evaluation
			Sheets	

Summary

In this chapter we showed the process of mapping out a current Learning Path. The easy part of mapping out the path is to capture the formal training that is currently happening. The more challenging part will be to determine what happens during an informal coaching or probationary period and the time when no formal training happens and yet proficiency hasn't been reached.

In addition, it's not all that uncommon to find that there is really no Learning Path or that there are several. Through the process of mapping out a Learning Path, the Learning Path Team will be able to establish a single Learning Path that will serve as a starting point for improvements.

The next chapter on Quick Hits starts the improvement process. However, in the process of establishing baseline measures and mapping out the Learning Path for the first time, you should already have a substantial list of ideas for improvement. At this point in time, you should still be within the initial thirty days and you will soon have a revised Learning Path that is significantly shorter.

5

Finding Quick Hits

REMEMBER ALL THOSE great improvement ideas that you generated while working on your Learning Path? Now you are ready to
tackle them. We want to start with Quick Hits. A Quick Hit is anything that
is relatively simple, low cost, and easily implemented. In addition, it needs
to be something that happens fast. Generating quick results will build and
sustain momentum for the much larger, time-consuming, and costly process
of accelerating a Learning Path. Let's set an arbitrary time limit on any Quick
Hit of thirty days or less.

Keep in mind that as you search for Quick Hits there are two different
places to look. First, consider revising and improving everything up to
Graduation Day. This really involves revising, updating, and improving the
existing training. Second, look at what's been happening in the mystery
period between Graduation and Independence Day. Look for ways to formalize that learning and add it into the formal training. (See Figure 5.1.)

Figure 5.1. Searching for Quick Hits

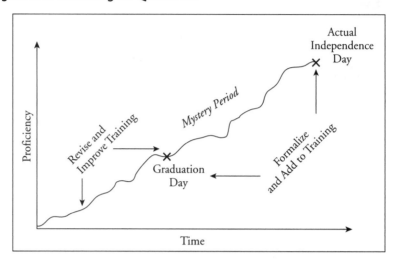

Working on Quick Hits is a great team activity. Your Learning Path Team should be eager and ready to get to the next step. Let's go through the basic Quick Hit ideas.

Out with the Old Stuff

As you go through each line item on your Learning Path, you may see training that is no longer needed. The training was built five years ago and you no longer use a number of the processes listed. You may find some old reports and manual processes that have not been automated.

What else could you find? How about training on products that used to be big sellers that are now on closeout? Any laws that have changed that outdate old policies and procedures? You may even find that no one has taken out all the old policies and procedures. They were just left in, along with the new ones.

There will also be some obvious duplication, especially if different parts of the training were developed by different people at different times. It's very easy for two different presenters to give an industry overview. In this respect, you should also look for any contrary or contradicting material, in other words, two very different views of the industry.

There may also be some information that is either unnecessary or simply overkill. You could easily have more information about the industry and its history than even the VP of marketing would need to know. Another great example of this is when you are working internationally and you teach more about the customer's country, culture, and history than the new customers would know. If you ask those around your office who knows the name of the fifteenth vice president of the United States, you're not likely to get a correct answer. Why would someone in the Philippines need to know that? Yet it sometimes shows up in training.

So if it's unnecessary, redundant, wrong, out-of-date, or just not worth the time, then draw a big red line through it on your Learning Path. This is a step that you will continue to do as part of Learning Path maintenance because what needs to be in training evolves at a different rate than building it does. Until everything is revised in real time, a lot of stuff needs the axe.

Tests and Milestones

There has to be an adequate way to monitor progress as new employees go through a Learning Path. You need to be able to track everyone's progress so you can spot anything that slows things down. This means adding tests and milestones, if they aren't already there. Tests aren't just paper-and-pencil exams, although you do need to check on what people know and don't know.

Tests can be in the form of direct observation, call evaluations, simulations, and written or oral presentations. You need to be able to test what people know and are able to do. You want to look at knowledge and behavior. In your Learning Path, look for places to add tests and decide how you will be able to collect and track those results.

We like to involve leaders as guides and coaches in this area. Consider doing structured interviews where the employee's manager asks prepared questions or observes specific activities and lets the employee know if he or she is ready to move forward on the Learning Path. We also recommend regular monitoring by the boss of the boss to make sure that proper coaching is taking place. This often involves training or coaching the coaches.

Milestones, on the other hand, are major progress points. Some people like to use the term "Toll Gates" instead. At each milestone, new employees need to pass a certain number of tests and produce a preset level of results. If the end goal involves doing one hundred transactions per day, as the employee progresses there should be a time when he or she will be able to do twenty-five, then fifty, and then seventy-five transactions per day.

Take a look at your Learning Path and try to draw a line where major milestones can be placed. Use actual data from existing employees, if possible. Write in what the milestone is and how it will be measured with feedback to the employee and the supervisor.

If finding enough eligible candidates for hire is a challenge, consider creating a Learning Path that concludes with proficiencies required to be hired. Once you have the basic Learning Path laid out, you may want to make an arrangement with an institute or school to develop and deliver the training for a fee paid by the potential employee.

Pre-Hire

While a Learning Path starts on Day One, there are a lot of things that can happen pre-hire to speed things up. One of the easiest things to do is to change the hiring profile. Instead of teaching certain skills, you just hire for them. However, you may be challenged to find enough employees who have the extra skills you want at the price you want to pay. In a situation where you are hiring hundreds of new employees in a short period of time, changing the hiring profile probably isn't realistic. Nevertheless, it's worth looking at.

We also talked a little bit already about exposing new employees to the reality of the job earlier. Moving that effort into pre-hire has the potential of screening out some of the new employees who would ordinarily quit in the first few weeks. For example, a lot of manufacturing plants are noisy and sometimes dark places to work. Many require wearing hard hats and ear plugs all day long. If you were working in circuit assembly in the past, you might think that most manufacturing environments are rather clean and quiet places. Well, you'd be wrong. So taking prospective new employees out on the shop floor for a few hours with a hard hat and ear plugs will help them decide if they really want to work in that environment.

In some cases, you can require some training as a pre-condition of hire. In these cases, you should have a partner, perhaps a community college, that can provide this education. Here are two examples of how this might work: At the lower end of the wage scale, you may be hiring new employees who lack some basic work skills even as simple as knowing that you need to show up for work every day on time and appropriately dressed.

To address this, many community colleges offer work readiness training or will work with you to build this type of program. If a new employee is starting in ten days, he or she would be required to go through this training, which might last two or three days.

There are also a lot of basic skills like word processing or building a spreadsheet that can be picked up through a class offered by a community college, or even a computer store. It's a matter of saying that, before you start, we'd like you to take this class. Keep in mind that developing new training takes time and can be very expensive, so if generic training can be purchased at a reasonable price it should be considered.

Add Coaching and Mentoring

The most meaningful way to speed up a Learning Path is to increase the involvement of managers and supervisors in the learning process. This means adding structured coaching and mentoring and not just writing it down in the blank spaces.

To make this happen, you may need to add training for managers and supervisors in coaching and mentoring. If these programs already exist, tailor these courses to coaching and mentoring with Learning Paths.

If you have a large number of employees in this function, this means you will have a large number of managers and supervisors. It's critical to get them all on the same page. Schedule regular meetings of about an hour with these managers and supervisors and discuss how coaching should be done and address any common challenges. The ultimate goal of these meetings is to make sure that managers and supervisors are coaching the same things in the same way.

Job Aids

Job aids are great substitutes and/or reinforcers for training. Job aids include:

- Checklists

- Evaluation sheets

- Cheat sheets

- Grids and matrices

- Online help

- Reference manuals

- Banners and posters

Job aids help new employees remember key information or provide quick access to information they will use all the time. Job aids don't have to be permanent. One tool that's very effective in a call center is reminder cards.

A reminder card might be as simple as a 3-inch by 5-inch card that has the standard greeting in big letters. Once you have the greeting memorized and remember to use it, you throw the card out.

Implementation

At the end of the Quick Hit process, you will have a revised Learning Path that is ready for implementation. As you do the implementation, it's important to continue the measurement process so that you can measure the actual change to Time to Proficiency. This new real data will help you report your results and justify your Learning Path Initiative.

If you are following the 30/30 Plan (Figure 5.2), you should reach the implementation step within the first thirty days. From here you can choose to work on additional functions or continue on by accelerating this Learning Path even more.

Figure 5.2. 30/30 Plan

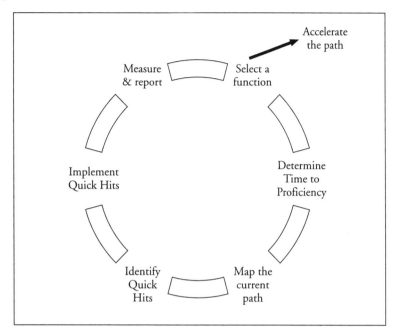

Accelerate
the path

Measure
& report

Select a
function

Implement
Quick Hits

Determine
Time to
Proficiency

Identify
Quick
Hits

Map the
current
path

CASE STUDY: PART 4

Now let's go back and look at the Quick Hits that GII identified. In this process, the team will be looking for ways to reduce the time between the end of the nesting period and proficiency.

In addition, the team has started to move a lot of the classroom presentations into directed self-study. These tend to be long and boring. The information is useful but not critical. The team is also looking at how to move some of the customer systems and technical training to on-the-job training. Finally, they want to provide a lot more structure to the nesting period. This will require doing some coaches' training for the supervisors and leads.

The example in Exhibit 5.1 shows just the first round of Quick Hits. The team is also going to go back into the training materials page-by-page and look for what can be deleted or needs to be updated.

Finally, the team can now create and implement a revised Learning Path that should be significantly faster than the current path. As seen in Exhibit 5.2, the team has reduced the actual classroom time as well as added more practice to make the on-the-job training more effective. Sometimes we find that the classroom or formal training increases. The important results are the reduction in the mystery period and arriving at Independence Day sooner.

Once this new Learning Path is implemented, they can measure Time to Proficiency again to see the actual reduction in time. You'll see in Exhibit 5.2 that the team cut classroom training from fifteen to twelve days. However, they decided to devote the three days they saved to additional nesting time. They added a lot more detail about the nesting time. The team felt that the extra time on the job would get CSRs up-to-speed faster. The team was able to route calls so that the three major types of calls, inquiries, order taking, and problems, could be worked on in sequence.

Exhibit 5.1. Quick Hits Action Plan Example

Quick Hits	How	Who	When
Add more hands-on experience during the first two weeks	- Add one hour of call observation on Days 3, 5, 7, and 9 - Attend weekly team meetings to hear how problems are addressed	Karen	11/1
Reduce classroom time spent on department presentations	- Capture presentations and transform them into directed self-study - Insert the new self-study into the nesting period	Kathy	11/16
Move learning the phone system out of the classroom	- Build a quick coaching guide that will enable CSR leads to quickly teach the phone system during an observation session	Kathy	11/12
Remove training on the GII - Galaxy	- Product support has been moved out of customer service to the distributors	Kathy	11/11
Create virtual tours of the plant and warehouse	- Use a digital video camera and walk through the facilities with the plant manager and warehouse manager. In-person tours can be scheduled later, as needed	Alice	11/1
Develop a formal process for the nesting period	- Establish proficiency measures - Create new call monitoring sheets for new employees - Provide coaches training for leads	Kathy	11/3
Continue the nesting period until proficiency is reached.	- Extend practice and review activities on an individual basis until proficiency is reached	Kathy	11/12

Exhibit 5.2. Case Study Revised Learning Path

Function: _____CSR_____   *Date:* _2/02/03_

Day	What	How	Materials	Done
1	New employee orientation - Welcome - Company history, goals, and mission - Product overview - Competition - Work rules - HR paperwork - Benefits - Customer service and your role Virtual Tours - Plant tour - Warehouse tour - Customer service center	Classroom	Leader's Guide Workbook Overheads New Employee Orientation Manual HR Benefits Package Virtual Tour CD Student Guide	
2	CSE (Customer Service Excellence Software Program) - Log on/log off - Finding a customer record - Change of information - Practice	Classroom	Leader's Guide Workbook Overheads	
3	CSE (Continued) - Setting up a new customer - Checking on order status - Adding journal entries - Sending emails - Practice	Classroom	Overheads Handouts	
4	CSE (Continued) - Taking a new order - Checking billing status - Practice	Classroom	Leader's Guide Workbook Overheads	
5	CSE (Continued) - Sending promotional material - Doing price quotes - Scheduling a new order - Practice	Classroom	Leader's Guide Workbook Overheads	
6	CSE (Continued) - Review and practice	Classroom	Leader's Guide Workbook Overheads	

Day	What	How	Materials	Done
7	Product Presentations – GII - Neptune – GII - Saturn – GII - Jupiter	Classroom	Overheads Handouts	
8	Customer Service Skills – Taking new orders – Handling problems and complaints – Role play and practice	Classroom	Leader's Guide Workbook Overheads	
9	Using the Phone System – Features – Logging in and out – Call transfers – Three-way calling – Conferencing – Practice – Telephone etiquette	On the Job	Reference Guide Coaching Guide	
10	Communication Skills – Listening – Business writing – Interpersonal styles	Classroom	Leader's Guide Workbook Overheads	
11	Team Building – Sending promotional material – Doing price quotes – Scheduling a new order – Practice	Classroom	Leader's Guide Workbook Overheads	
12	Call Handling Practice – Observation and role play – Graduation	Classroom	Leader's Guide Workbook Overheads	
13	*Nesting Starts* – Phone system orientation by supervisor – Inquiry call observation and practice with a Lead CSR – Observe 5 calls – Take 15 calls and get feedback – Discuss and evaluate learning from the day	On the Job	Nesting Reference Guide Call Evaluation Sheets Coaching Guide	

Day	What	How	Materials	Done
14	Customer Service Department Self-Study 1 Hr. Continue Inquiry Call Practice - Take 15 calls - Supervisor observes and gives feedback on 5 calls - Discuss and evaluate learning from the day	Self-Study On the Job	Self-Study Reading Assignment Coaching Guide	
15	Continue Inquiry Call Practice - Take 15 calls - Supervisor observes and gives feedback on 5 calls - Discuss and evaluate learning from the day	On the Job	Coaching Guide	
16	Marketing Department Self-Study 1 Hr. Continue Inquiry Call Practice - Take 15 calls - Supervisor observes and gives feedback on 5 calls - Discuss and evaluate learning from the day	Self-Study On the Job	Self-Study Reading Assignment	
17	Performance Evaluation by Supervisor New Order Call Observation and Practice with a Lead CSR - Observe 5 calls - Take 15 calls and get feedback - Discuss and evaluate learning from the day	On the Job On the Job	Performance Evaluation Coaching Guide	
18	Sales Department Self-Study 1 Hr. Continue New Order Call Practice - Take 15 calls - Supervisor observes and gives feedback on 5 calls - Discuss and evaluate learning from the day	Self-Study On the Job	Self-Study Reading Assignment	
19	Continue New Order Call Practice - Take 15 calls - Supervisor observes and gives feedback on 5 calls - Discuss and evaluate learning from the day	On the Job	Coaching Guide	

Day	What	How	Materials	Done
20	Production Department Self-Study 1 Hr. Practice Both Inquiry and New Order Calls	Self-Study On the Job	Self-Study Reading Assignment Coaching Guide	
21	Practice Both Inquiry and New Order Call Performance Evaluation by Supervisor	On the Job	Coaching Guide Performance Evaluation	
22	Engineering Department Self-Study 1 Hr. Problem Call Observation and Practice with a Lead CSR - Observe 5 calls - Take 15 calls and get feedback - Discuss and evaluate learning from the day	Self-Study On the Job	Self-Study Reading Assignment	
23	Sales Department Self-Study 1 Hr. Continue Problem Call Practice - Take 15 calls - Supervisor observes and gives feedback on 5 calls - Discuss and evaluate learning from the day	Self-Study On the Job	Self-Study Reading Assignment Coaching Guide	
24	Continue Problem Call Practice - Take 15 calls - Supervisor observes and gives feedback on 5 calls - Discuss and evaluate learning from the day	On the Job	Coaching Guide	
25	All Call Practice and Observation	On the Job	Coaching Guide	
26	Distribution Department Self-Study 1 Hr. All Call Practice and Observation	Self-Study On the Job	Self-Study Reading Assignment	
27	All Call Practice and Observation	On the Job	Coaching Guide	
28	All Call Practice and Observation	On the Job	Coaching Guide	
29	All Call Practice and Observation	On the Job	Coaching Guide	
30	Final Evaluation by Supervisor – Learning Path Extended if Needed	On the Job	Final Test and Performance Evaluation	

Thirty-Day Report

At the end of the Quick Hits process, you should be at about thirty days in your development timeline. This is an excellent time to report the progress your team has made, including your planned reduction in Time to Proficiency. Figures 5.3 through 5.8 provide an example of a Thirty-Day Sales Report, beginning with a cover sheet.

Figure 5.4 shows the activity that is normally completed within the first thirty days. However, for some functions it may take longer to implement all of the Quick Hits. Figure 5.5 introduces the proficiency measures for the selected functions. If data is available, you may also want to include information about the difference between average and top performers. Figure 5.6 shows three views of Time to Proficiency. First, it shows the actual measure of the current Learning Path. Second, if a survey was done, it shows the estimated Time to Proficiency. Third, it shows the planned length of time of the new Learning Path. Once this path has been implemented and measured, there will be a new actual Time to Proficiency. Figure 5.7 is a recap of the major Quick Hits that were identified and incorporated into the new

Figure 5.3. Cover Sheet

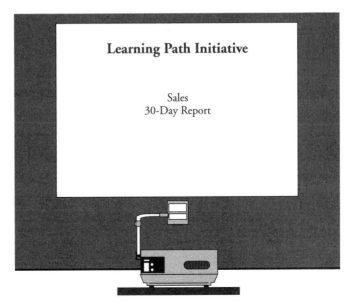

Learning Path Initiative

Sales
30-Day Report

Learning Path. Notice that it includes increases in practice and testing. Figure 5.8 shows what will be happening after the presentation. The key next

Figure 5.4. Thirty-Day Activity Summary

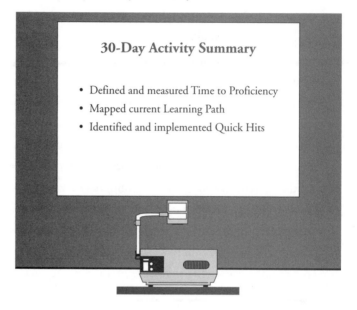

Figure 5.5. Proficiency Measures

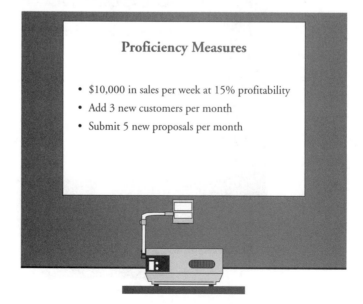

step is always the implementation and measurement of the new Learning Path. In many cases, you may also be going on to reengineer this path.

Figure 5.6. Time to Proficiency

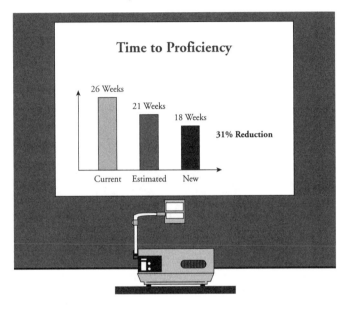

Figure 5.7. Quick Hits Summary

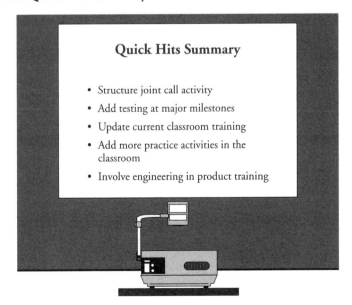

Figure 5.8. Next Steps

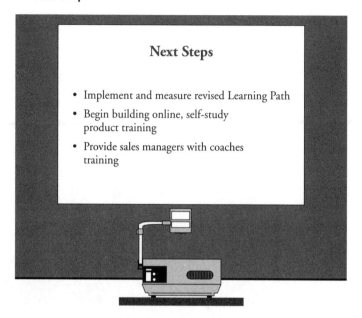

(Note that there is a blank presentation template on the CD that you can use to customize this report for your own Learning Path Initiative.)

Summary

Once you've gone through the rigor of measuring Time to Proficiency and mapping out a Learning Path, there usually are a large number of obvious improvements that can be made. Some of those improvements come from making the classroom training more effective and relevant. However, working on improvement from the time training ends until proficiency is achieved will shorten the Learning Path the fastest.

With a concerted and focused effort, most Learning Path Teams can have a revised Learning Path ready to implement within thirty days. In the next chapter, we will be looking at making further improvements to a Learning Path by applying a range of accelerated learning principles and really reengineering the Learning Path, rather than just changing it. Many of the ideas in the next chapter will also help you with Quick Hits as you begin to work on other functions.

6

Accelerating Learning Paths

THE LAST TWO CHAPTERS were focused on mapping out a current Learning Path that reflects everything that happened from Day One to Independence Day. From the current Learning Path, the Learning Path Team searched for and found ways to improve and shrink the path through Quick Hits. The end result was a revised Learning Path.

In this chapter we are going to look at creating a third version of the Learning Path that will be different from the other two. We will be looking at ways to completely reengineer the Learning Path so that it not only shrinks the time between Day One and Independence Day but also closes the gap between Graduation and Independence Day.

Everything that was done up to this point can be completed within the first thirty days. Since reengineering a Learning Path will require considerable changes to the training, this step will take a lot longer and may have to be done in phases, as shown in Figure 6.1.

Figure 6.1. Accelerated Learning Path

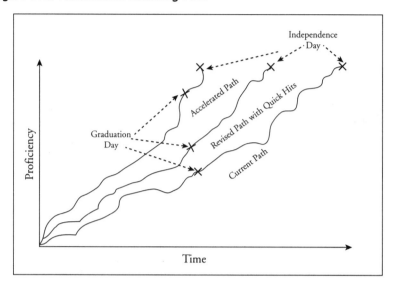

Applying Learning Principles

In Chapter 1, we talked about how people really learn. We said that it is more than just a series of classroom training programs. It includes practice and experience. In the simplest form, just laying out a Learning Path and making sure everyone follows it will speed up the learning process. It will also lead to a greater degree of consistency in how each new person is trained.

The first, and probably the most important, step in speeding up a Learning Path is to agree on a set of Learning Principles that can then be applied consistently across a Learning Path. When setting out these principles, keep an eye on driving down training costs while increasing what we call the "Stick Factor." The Stick Factor relates to making sure that training is remembered, used, and reinforced by managers for days, months, and years after the training. Have you ever gone through a training seminar that you thought was informative, motivating, and entertaining and then, a week later, you couldn't remember much about it? That's very common because the training lacked the Stick Factor.

Just an aside, in this book we use the terms learning, training, and education. At times we use them interchangeably. In the learning/training/ education community, there are always debates about which is the best to use and which is more precise. We think that it's always a good idea to use common terms and definitions, but don't spend too much time on it. There are better things to do.

To model the same process we use to build a lot of training, we are going to present a set of accelerated Learning Principles for you to consider. With your team you can modify, change, add, or delete anything to create your own set of principles.

Principle #1: Managers Need to Be Trainers

Managers must be aware of and support any training in order for it to be effective. However, it's not uncommon for a manager to contradict what happens in training. Managers often feel that the training is too theoretical, not the way they were trained, or out-of-date.

This happens because they were not involved in the building or the delivery of training. To address this, managers must be trainers or at least be paired up with a training professional. This also means that any training has to be developed for managers to deliver, and managers may also need training in how to be trainers.

Having managers as trainers can lead to tremendous cost savings in environments where there are small numbers of people in remote locations, such as in branch sales offices. As we determine how to deliver training, we need to select methods that will fit with managers' capabilities and time frames. We can't usually plan on them spending three weeks in the classroom with new hires.

Here are two quick examples of how you would change a training program to make it more manager-friendly. Let's start with a basic sales training program, which is often taught in a three- to five-day workshop. All the content and formats are laid out with easy instructions for the manager. The more detailed and easy to use the materials are, the more likely they are to be used, and used in a more consistent way from one manager to the next. You take the same content and break it up into a series of twenty- to thirty-minute sales meetings. After each sales meeting there are field activities where salespeople try to apply what they've learned. At the start of each sales meeting there is always a review of what happened in the field.

These meetings are then spread out with two or three a week over a period of about six weeks. What happens is that sales managers end up spending a lot of time working with salespeople in a structured coaching environment. As a result, management support goes up, along with the Stick Factor.

Let's take a second example where one of the tasks is to inspect vehicles when they are returned from a lease. Here the content is delivered by a directed, self-study reading assignment or even a short e-learning lesson. This gives the new person a basic background on how to do an inspection. Then the new person and the manager go out and do inspections together. The manager is given a guide on how to do this on-the-job training. This goes quickly because the manager doesn't need to lecture on the basics. That was already covered in the self-study.

Applying this first principle, consider using managers as a first choice in training delivery and development. Use training professionals to lead the process and develop Learning Paths, including one for leaders to become coaches and mentors. We believe training is leadership.

Principle #2: Reserve Classroom Time for Practice and Discussion

Classroom time is expensive. It's particularly expensive when travel is involved. One of the fastest ways to drive down the cost of training is to reduce the amount of training that is done in classrooms.

A great majority of classroom time is spent with lectures and presentations. If you've ever spent eight hours watching an instructor run through a mountain of PowerPoint® slides, you're really going to like applying this principle. When you have to go through weeks of classroom training, not only do you remember very little of it, but it's also punishing.

We recommend that you take anything related to knowledge acquisition and transform it into self-study. We will talk more about how to do this in later chapters. When you do go into the classroom, you can quickly review the content and go on to discussion and application.

Here's one method we have used very successfully to move to this type of a model. Start with an existing training program that has a leader's guide, participant's guide, and overheads. This is very typical of most training programs. Let's assume we are dealing with a problem-solving class. Cut and paste all of the content into a reading assignment. This involves some reformatting and writing of transitions. A good writer can do this in a day or two.

Add tests and a few field activities to help the student understand and remember the content. You now have the self-study assignment, which will be the prework for the class. Anything you didn't reformat into self-study should be used for discussion and application. If there isn't any, you might not need the class.

However, your new classroom session should apply what the students read about to a series of problems. The instructor spends the entire time helping and coaching the participants through these problems. This is something a manager can probably do better than a trainer because of his or her practical knowledge about these types of problems. You also don't need someone with great presentation skills because you eliminated the lectures. A professional trainer may teach the business leader to conduct the classroom session, which will be mostly activities with structured evaluation and feedback. This is a great opportunity to teach leaders the basics of coaching. The professional trainer's job is then to make sure the manager has everything needed for success.

Principle #3: All Self-Study Needs to Be Directed Self-Study

One criticism of self-study in all its forms, from print to e-learning, is that people just won't do it. It's a valid statement, if you just give someone a book and say, "Read it when you have time." However, when we talk about self-study we mean what we call *directed* self-study. Directed self-study means all of the following:

- It's an integral part of a Learning Path. You can't get through the Learning Path without completing the self-study.

- The manager or coach is required to review and discuss every self-study assignment, and written directions are provided for the manager or coach with each assignment.

- There are tests with each self-study assignment that are reviewed and monitored. These are also used to monitor progress through the Learning Path.

- Self-study assignments are usually used as prework for classroom sessions or to provide content immediately before on-the-job training.

In addition to these specifics, there are other methods of making self-study more effective. They include:

- Schedule a time and provide a place to work on the self-study.

- Create incentives and rewards for completing self-study assignments.

- Use multiple methods of delivering self-study to make it more user-friendly. We like to use the book on tape approach, with a print and an audio version of any program.

After applying the first three principles, a Learning Path starts to look significantly different. Blocks of classroom training are being transformed into a mixture of self-study, on-the-job training, and modified classroom training. Knowledge is delivered in self-study. Classroom training is reserved for discussion and practice. Managers make sure everything transfers to the job.

Principle #4: Teach the Whole Job, Not Parts

Traditionally, training has been taught in a topic-by-topic, building-block approach. You usually end up with a sequence of topics that looks like this:

- Company Overview
- Industry/Market Overview
- Product Characteristics

- Computer Applications

- Sales Process

- Putting It All Together

This approach is the easiest for someone to design and develop and it's also a good, analytical way to think about training. However, it's not how people really learn, and it doesn't reflect how the job is actually done. For example, if you're on the phone taking reservations, you need to use the phone, your computer, and a reservations process all at once. If you learn them piece by piece, you still don't know how to use them together.

This new approach requires that you identify each of the major types of reservation calls and then sequence them from easy to complex. You then teach the computer, phone, and process for each call. Students practice each type of call until it's mastered and then move on to the next call.

You might have already made the link with the last principle. There's no reason a learner can't do some self-study on a call type just prior to doing practice activities with an instructor, who could easily be a manager. We have found that this approach can work with any job at any level.

In Chapter 9 on Building Proficiency Models, this concept is explored in more detail. We look at the importance of identifying how jobs are really done as a basis for building a Learning Path. You'll see that one of the things that slows down a Learning Path the fastest is the separation of "technical" and "soft" skills. For example, a computer technician is taught how to fix a computer and then may go through a customer service course. But the real skill needed is to be able to talk with the customer while fixing the computer in a way that builds confidence and customer loyalty. It's similar to the physician who knows how to practice medicine but has a lousy bedside manner. This happens because the skill of dealing with patients isn't taught in conjunction with the technical aspects of medicine.

So any Learning Path that looks like a curriculum with a series of topics can be accelerated by reorienting the Learning Path around a logical sequence of tasks, functions, and processes. Usually the best way to sequence these tasks is from simple to complex.

Principle #5: Require Mastery, Not Participation

When there is testing, there is always a discussion about what is a satisfactory or passing grade. Should it be 70 percent, 85 percent, or should it be 100 percent? Let's say that you set a target of 75 percent. That means that you are allowing for 25 percent mistakes or errors. That's a very large number. Over a long series of training events, that adds up to a tremendous amount that participants don't know and won't be able to do. They may pick it up over time, but in essence you've wasted a lot of time and money.

Therefore, if something is really important to know and is job critical, you need to get as close to 100 percent as possible. Getting things right the first time does add speed to a Learning Path. It also makes you think about all the topics from which you would be willing to accept a lower score. Maybe they are really not that important and can be eliminated.

Paper-and-pencil tests are fine for testing knowledge, and some jobs do require a lot of knowledge recall. However, most jobs will require a higher level of testing, which involves direct observation and measurement of results. Evaluation by observation will become a lot easier as managers become more involved in training. Since they are often the experts, they know what to look for and can take corrective actions immediately. In addition, since we are already measuring Time to Proficiency, there is a measurement rigor that is also in place.

Finally, since the new path is structured around a sequence of tasks or processes, you will be testing proficiency in those tasks or processes. So as you re-map a Learning Path, the logical place to put rigorous testing is after each of these key pieces.

Principle #6: Connect to Business Needs

Note that Chapter 11 is devoted to this principle because we feel it's so important. However, we want to preview it here because it fits in the sequence of principles that will help you reengineer a Learning Path.

With that said, most training gets out-of-date because there is a lag between changes in the business and the development of new training. In most organizations, two things that allow training to be connected to current business needs on a real-time basis are missing. First, there is no formal and continuous process for identifying business needs and how they will relate to training. Second, there is no process for updating training in real time.

We recommend undertaking Business Needs Analysis sessions with senior management. These sessions should dovetail with the existing business planning process and provide an opportunity to focus on training needs. We recommend an annual session for each major business area. A quarterly update session will be needed to keep up with the pace of change in most businesses today. We have devoted a later chapter to describing how to conduct one of these sessions. In essence, the leadership team looks at current business issues and future business needs and then looks at the impact that both of these will have on the workforce.

For example, in one of these sessions there might be an in-depth discussion about customer comments, complaints, and suggestions. This might lead to changes in how front-line employees interact with customers, which in turn creates a change in the training for these employees.

There may be discussions about moving a function to a different location or adding more employees and putting them in a new location. Now there is the great challenge of replicating what's being done, which in turn leads to the need to evaluate and change any training so that it is portable.

As businesses struggle to be more agile and change quickly, this puts pressure on the training function to respond and react as close to real time as possible. This involves looking at how training is developed and perhaps changing the delivery methods or instructional strategy so that you can add and drop elements without affecting the overall flow of the training. And it means refining the review and production processes so that they also move as quickly as possible.

Principle #7: Embrace Technology

Technology has added speed and productivity to everyone's business function. However, training has been historically slow to adopt and figure out how to use technology. Just take a look at a typical PowerPoint training lecture. Almost all of them use only a small percentage of the features of PowerPoint.

You still see the "bean people," which were some of the first clip art used with PowerPoint ten years ago. e-learning and Web-based training are part of the technology solution, but others can be extremely powerful. These technologies include screen captures, digital video, speech recognition, teleconferences/video conferences, and online meeting forums. In Chapter 12 on Capturing Content, you will find a more detailed explanation of these technologies and examples of how they can be used.

For those of us who worked as instructional designers before PCs, we remember how difficult it was to create professional-looking training documents. Everything had to be typed, so if you wanted to make a change you had to retype the entire document. As a result, you were slow or resistant to making changes. Most organizations have been slow to use a lot of video because it was always expensive and difficult to change. However, with digital videocameras, you can make a lot of good-looking videos that can be part of training the same day. It's critical to keep a constant eye on technology in respect to increasing speed and driving down costs.

Principle #8: Quantity Versus Quality

In the push for quality, we often overlook the benefits of quantity. For example, when you decide to add video to training you have a decision to make. Do you spend a lot of time and money creating a limited amount of professional quality video or do you go out with your digital camera and create a large amount of video in an afternoon?

Let's assume that you are going to create a plant tour video for new employees. The purpose of this video is to show new employees what a typical day in the plant is like. A professional, fifteen-minute video with scripting, actors, and narration will take anywhere from thirty days to six months to get approved and shoot. The cost will be somewhere between $20,000 and $50,000.

You seldom see these videos updated because they weren't designed to be easily changed, since they typically have a continuous story. Also, setting up to re-shoot can be as expensive as the original video.

Here's a completely different approach. You take your digital camera. You ask the plant manager who gives plant tours to walk you through the plant. You stop at each piece of machinery and capture what the plant manager typically says. To make sure you capture the sound clearly, you use a $10 lapel microphone.

With a little experience with any desktop editing program, you can create a series of small digital videos that take you through the plant. When something changes, you can quickly shoot a new piece of video and drop that file into your presentation. If you want to step up the production values, you can strip out the audio and have a professional narrator restate what the plant manager said.

Unlike the old VHS camcorders, digital video gives you high-quality video without additional lighting or staging. And it doesn't look like the old home movies. Just imagine what might happen if digital camcorders were available for any department to create videos with current information that they wanted to share. Think about how that moves you to real time.

The point is that a focus on speed and quantity is going to take you closer to real-time training. The quality will start to pick up as everyone learns how to use the various pieces of technology and gets better at them. You might even want to create a Learning Path for developing training with new technology.

Principle #9: Use Design Templates

In focusing more strongly on generating a lot of real-time training, it's useful to make many of the instructional design decisions in advance. Take something as simple as a self-study reading assignment.

Each time you build one, you don't need to make decisions about the format, what typeface to use, how many words on a page, the writing style, or where and how many tests to put in. You can create a standard design template that can be filled in with the content.

Templates can be created for all types of training, from workshops to videos. These templates will reduce everyone's time thinking about style and direct them to concentrate on substance. We've found it very helpful to create a Learning Path and training around developing training that imbeds these templates in to all training development.

Templates also have the effect of teaching the student how to go through any given piece of training. They will know what to expect and what to do without a lot of instruction. Again, faster training development will lead to training that is more timely and useful, which in turn will accelerate Learning Paths.

Principle #10: Make Content King—Write It Down

In a typical organization, most of the content exists in the head of an expert. It's not readily available or usable by anyone other than the expert. Again, we go back to the stack of PowerPoint slides and the expert talking us through each one.

What happens when the expert leaves or isn't available? Obviously, the content goes along with the expert. What we also see a lot is that businesses want to move from traditional training to some type of e-learning. The problem is that e-learning tools are just empty templates. You can't take the stack of PowerPoint slides and make them into an online lesson. You have to capture the expert content, which is almost never written down.

Making the change from classroom training with experts making presentations to some other methodology requires that you start writing things down. A lot of good tools are available that can help with content capture, but no matter how you do it, it's critical to begin with writing things down.

One of the new trends in e-learning is to use an objects approach and to build a database of the organization's knowledge. While the technology works really well, the big stumbling block is that, if the content isn't written down in the first place, you can't put it in a database.

The same holds true for a learning management system, also called an LMS. These are great tools for tracking and scheduling training. However, it's like getting a new toy without the batteries. What's missing in an LMS is the content. What you will find as you build Learning Paths is that the Learning Path actually becomes the structure and content that goes into the LMS to make it work.

Principle #11: Use Proficiencies Versus Competencies

We started out trying to identify and verify what should be in a Learning Path by creating a competency model and then trying to match the two up. However, we found that wasn't enough. In a traditional competency model, you are trying to find the skills, knowledge, and attitudes, or sometimes attributes, required to perform a job or function.

While competency models may be fine and appropriate for training, we need to be a lot more specific and measurable to be useful for Learning Paths. First of all, when you look at examples of competency models, they all look different. Some have one hundred competencies, while others have only ten for the same function. Sometimes, they look like a laundry list of topics, especially when you look at knowledge competencies. Others start to look like learning objectives.

What's more useful is to ask the following questions:

- What are the major tasks or processes for this job?
- What combinations of skill, knowledge, and attitudes are needed for each major task or process to achieve desired results?
- What are the desired results?
- What are the standards of acceptable results?

For new employees, the desired result is going to be performing these functions or tasks at an independently productive level with average output.

Let's look at an easy competency area for a salesperson. Let's take prospecting or finding new business. What's basically needed in prospecting is that you can find good leads, qualify them, and have the discipline to work on prospecting on a regular basis. In this effort, the salesperson needs to be able to use a computer to find new prospects online and to track prospecting efforts in a sales management system. He or she may also need some phone skills to do qualifying and maybe even set up an appointment.

In this description, we have included organizational skills, phone skills, voice skills, planning skills, analytical skills, computer application skills, knowledge about prospects and qualifying criteria, how to set an appointment, and how to sustain the overall discipline to go at it every day. The overriding competency is that you must be able to do all this at the same time and not sequentially.

So under a general heading of "Prospecting," a proficiency might be

- Identifying and qualifying sufficient new business leads to get five new appointments per week

- Using the sales management system daily to plan and monitor new business activity

Again, we are looking at how things fit together rather than listing all the parts. We are going to try to build training that reflects how jobs are really done, rather than just the pieces and parts.

Principle #12: Motivation

One of the most forgotten parts of training is focusing on motivation. In the learning process, there are a lot of peaks and valleys in motivation. Usually, when we are having a lot of successes our motivation is up and when we are struggling, our motivation—and often our confidence—goes down.

While we want to have all of the awards, certificates, contests, and incentives with any training, we also want to build in some of the key elements that will keep participants motivated. Here are some key motivational tips:

- Make training relevant to the job.

- Get to working on the actual job as quickly as possible.

- Make sure coaches and mentors are available to provide support when there are problems.
- Make training active and participatory.
- Avoid endless hours in the classroom.
- Build in activities where participants can be successful.
- Recognize and support successes.
- Don't punish anyone during training. Allow people to make mistakes and learn from those mistakes.
- Use a wide range of media and techniques.
- Make it fun but make it meaningful.

Let's go back and look at our Learning Path and talk about how you apply these principles in some structured, logical manner. We know you're going to have trouble applying all of these principles immediately and at the same time. Each Learning Path will have different areas of need, but here is one approach you might try.

1. Reduce Classroom Time

Look at each item on your Learning Path that is marked "classroom training." Transform everything that is lecture-based into a self-study reading assignment. Once you've done this, ask if you still need that classroom time.

2. Replace Classroom with On-the-Job Practice

If you have the content in a self-study reading assignment, you may be able to do the practice and application on the job with a coach. Remember our example about inspections. When we combined a self-study with on-the-job training we didn't need any classroom time. But don't forget to structure and monitor the on-the-job part to make sure it really happens.

3. Replace Training with Job Aids

Go back through the Learning Path again and try to find anything that could also be done through a job aid. Instead of a question-and-answer session in the classroom, maybe all you need is an online help area.

4. Look for Combinations

Now you are starting to get into more complex redesign. When you look at the topic-by-topic approach, look for ways to combine these topics together to reflect how a job is done. It will help to have good process maps for each job and to have identified the major tasks so that you can make these combinations.

5. Re-Sequence

What we are looking for as we re-sequence is to try to arrange the training around common tasks, going from simple to complex. We are trying to build in a pathway of success and to simulate in training how the job is done.

6. Reuse

Any number of Learning Paths may have common elements. Find the best and dump the rest. This is particularly true with generic training such as presentation skills or business writing. But even the business-specific training may be used on multiple Learning Paths. The basics of the insurance industry and an overview of the product line are not only important to application processors and claims processors.

Those are the basic techniques for accelerating a Learning Path. In the next several chapters we will go into more detail on how to put these ideas and concepts into action. As we've said, laying out a Learning Path and accomplishing gains with Quick Hits can be completed within thirty days. But accelerating a Learning Path is really a continuous improvement process where you will see the gains grow over time.

As a final note, keep in mind that we are trying to close the gap between Graduation Day and Independence Day. In fact, our goal is to make them the same. This means that in reengineering a Learning Path, all learning activities have to be accounted for. This includes being very specific about the practice and experience required.

Learning Path Evaluation Checklist

To help apply these principles to a Learning Path, use the Learning Path Evaluation Checklist in Exhibit 6.1. You can also use it to identify additional ways to shorten a Learning Path.

Exhibit 6.1. Learning Path Evaluation

Factor	Rating	Required Actions
1. Information, policies and procedures are current, complete, and correct.	1 2 3 4 5	
2. Content has been moved from classroom delivery to self-study.	1 2 3 4 5	
3. Managers have assumed the role of coaches and direct all self-study.	1 2 3 4 5	
4. The Learning Path is sequenced around tasks, functions, and processes rather than topics.	1 2 3 4 5	
5. Tasks, functions, and processes are sequenced from simple to complex.	1 2 3 4 5	
6. Test and measurements are used to track progress along the Learning Path.	1 2 3 4 5	
7. The gap between Graduation Day and Independence Day has been closed.	1 2 3 4 5	
8. Practice and experience have been quantified and included in the Learning Path.	1 2 3 4 5	
9. Each line item has been evaluated to make sure it is the most appropriate way to deliver that training.	1 2 3 4 5	
10. Strategies are in place to keep employees motivated and engaged.	1 2 3 4 5	

CASE STUDY: PART 5

While the revised Learning Path with the Quick Hits was being implemented, the Learning Path Team decided to go ahead and reengineer their Learning Path. As a result of several planning meetings, the team decided on the following ways to accelerate their Learning Path.

- All of the calls could be grouped into five major call types: general inquiries, new orders, order status, product questions, and other problems.

- The phone system could be modified so these calls could be routed in any configuration.

- The training would be reorganized around these call types. CSRs would be expected to learn each call type and get to proficiency before moving on to the next one.

- The sequence of calls would be from simple to complex.

- CSRs would learn about the computer and the products as they related to each call.

- Coaching materials and processes would be rewritten and geared toward these call types.

Exhibit 6.2 shows the start of their accelerated Learning Path. After a pilot test and measurement of the first class to go through this path, the path will be revised again.

Exhibit 6.2. Revised Learning Path for GII

Accelerated Learning Path

Function: _____CSR_____   *Date:* _2/02/03_

Day	What	How	Materials	Done
1	New Employee Orientation – HR paperwork (Prior to starting class) – Benefits (Prior to starting class) – Welcome – Company history, goals, and mission – Product overview – Work rules – Customer service and your rules – Call observation	Classroom	Leader's Guide Workbook Overheads New Employee Manual HR Benefits Manual	
2	CSE Basics – Logging on and off – Navigating screens Inquiry Calls – Inquiry process – Frequent questions and answers – How to find answers (reference guide) – Transferring calls – Documenting the call	Classroom Classroom	Leader's Guide Workbook Overheads	
3	Inquiry Call Observation – Observing others – Asking questions Inquiry Call Practice – Take 25 calls with supervision Our Products	On the Job On the Job Self-Study	Coaching Guide Job Aids Coaching Guide Self-Study Reading Assignment	
4	Taking Inquiry Calls – Practice (25 calls) – Monitoring and feedback Department Self-Study	On the Job Self-Study	Coaching Guide Self-Study Reading Assignment	
5	Taking Inquiry Calls – Practice (25 calls) – Monitoring and feedback Plant and Warehouse Tours Self-Study	On the Job Self-Study	Coaching Guide Self-Study Reading Assignment	

Day	What	How	Materials	Done
6	New Order Calls – New order process – Pricing and product specs – Documenting the call	Classroom	Coaching Guide Job Aids	
7	New Order Call Observation – Observing others – Asking questions New Order Call Practice – Take 25 calls with supervision Manufacturing and Engineering	On the Job On the Job Self-Study	Coaching Guide Self-Study Reading Assignment	
8	Taking New Order Calls – Practice (25 calls) – Monitoring and feedback Customers and Competition Self-Study	On the Job Self-Study	Coaching Guide	
9	Taking New Order Calls – Practice (25 calls) – Monitoring and feedback Order Status Self-Study	On the Job Self-Study	Coaching Guide Self-Study Reading Assignment	
10	Order Status Call Observation – Observing others – Asking questions Order Status Call Practice – Take 25 calls with supervision	On the Job On the Job	Coaching Guide Job Aids	
11	Taking Order Status Calls – Practice (25 calls) – Monitoring and feedback	On the Job	Coaching Guide	
12	Taking Order Status Calls – Practice (25 calls) – Monitoring and feedback Product Questions Self-Study	On the Job Self-Study	Coaching Guide Self-Study Reading Assignment	
13	Product Questions Call Observation – Observing others – Asking questions Product Questions Call Practice – Take 25 calls with supervision	On the Job On the Job	Coaching Guide Job Aids Reference Manual	

Day	What	How	Materials	Done
14	Product Questions Calls - Practice (25 calls) - Monitoring and feedback	On the Job	Coaching Guide	
15	Product Questions Status Calls - Practice (25 calls) - Monitoring and feedback Handling Problems Self-Study	On the Job Self-Study	Coaching Guide Self-Study Reading Assignment	
16	Handling Problems Call Observation - Observing others - Asking questions Handling Problems Call Practice - Take 25 calls with supervision	On the Job On the Job	Coaching Guide	
17	Handling Problems Calls - Practice (25 calls) - Monitoring and feedback	On the Job	Coaching Guide	
18	Handling Problems Calls - Practice (25 calls) - Monitoring and feedback	On the Job	Coaching Guide	
19-25	Call Practice, Coaching and Monitoring (150 calls)	On the Job	Coaching Guide	
26	Final Testing and Evaluation. Continue coaching as needed on an individual basis.	On the Job	Coaching Guide Final Test and Evaluation	

Summary

One of the most important things for any organization to have is a set of learning principles that guides all the development and implementation of training. In this chapter, we've presented thirteen principles we've found to be highly effective. However, they are not meant to be every possible principle or strategy for instructional design. Other accelerated learning techniques have a place here, but it's impossible to cover them all.

The ultimate goal of this step in the Learning Path Methodology is to create a new Learning Path that better reflects how people really learn and covers the entire time period from Day One to Independence Day. Since this will generate more development work, this step will take longer than the Quick Hit process.

In addition, as you read through Parts II and III of this book, you will be presented with additional ways to work on and improve a Learning Path. In Part II, you will read about improving the connection between a Learning Path and business needs. In Part III, you will read about how to be more effective in the actual delivery of training.

7

Transition and Maintenance

WE'RE GOING TO assume that, at this point, you're well along the way to building Learning Paths, implementing Quick Hits, and developing new training. Soon you will be able to reduce classroom time and drive more training into one-on-one coaching situations. As you do this, you will be encountering two new issues: transition and maintenance.

Transition involves moving from what you have today, which is probably some type of curriculum approach, to a Learning Path approach. Because you will be implementing a Learning Path in stages, the transition will be gradual and staged rather than waiting until everything is done and turning on the switch. For example, if one of the Quick Hits is to delete all outdated information, you should make that change immediately and use revised materials for your next training class. In addition, if you intend to build twenty self-study reading assignments, you can introduce them as they are written rather than waiting until they are all finished.

In this chapter, we are going to look at transition planning and how to remove some of the key barriers that you should be able to anticipate. Remember that this is a major change initiative and that there will be some resistance as you go from the old to the new.

We are also going to look at maintenance. You are going to need to put some systems in place to make sure that measurement continues, materials are updated, and other improvements can be made. We'll be looking at developing a maintenance plan as well as at how to integrate a learning management system (LMS).

Transition Planning

The best way to understand the issues of transition planning is to look at the following example. Let's assume that we have built a Learning Path for a customer service call center. Before we started there was a new-hire class that also started meeting once a month. Classroom training lasted for two weeks, followed by a nesting period of four weeks. From our initial measurement, we found that, while the training lasted six weeks, customer service reps weren't Independently Productive until Week 9.

We now have the choice of building a Learning Path and revising all the training before we implement anything, or we can begin to implement pieces of the new training as they are developed. The benefit of waiting is that you can make a clean sweep of everything and avoid some of the confusion of installing new training piece-by-piece. The downside of waiting is that there are a lot of things that block or derail building of training, so it might take you a year before you can get everything together. We find that the best way to build and maintain support for this type of initiative is to build in early and frequent successes. In fact, we like to set a target of having a measurable change in the Time to Proficiency within the first thirty days.

Exhibit 7.1 is a transition plan from our example of a customer service center. Notice how it's divided into phases that will yield measurable improvements through the development cycle. Transitions issues are listed in Exhibit 7.2.

Exhibit 7.1. Sample Transition Plan

	Jan.	Feb.	March	April	May	June	July	Aug.	Sept.	Oct.	Nov.	Dec.
Phase 1: Measurement - Establish measures and measure each new group of new employees	X											
Phase 2: Map Out Current Learning Path - Train coaches on how to use the Learning Path during nesting period - Begin using the current Learning Path with new hires	X	X										
Phase 3: Measurement - Begin using revised training materials - Implement other Quick Hits		X X	X									
Phase 4: Build New Training - Replace classroom lectures with self-study reading assignments. 20 planned self-study reading assignments; replace them in batches of 5 - Install coaching tools and reference materials as they are developed - Pilot new group of employees and make revisions		X X	X X	X X	X X	X	X	X				
Phase 5: Roll-Out - Conduct roll out meeting - Conduct train-the-trainer - Coach coaches									X X X			

Exhibit 7.2. Sample Transition Issues Action Plan

Issues	Actions	Who	When
1. Building and maintaining management support	• Create and present monthly status reports • Present results of improvement in Time to Proficiency on a quarterly basis • Invite management to participate and observe training • Involve management in review cycle		
2. Building coaching and training skills to improve on-the-job training	• Hold kickoff meeting with coaches to explain the process • Establish weekly coaches' meetings • Provide updates and training as new coaching tools are built		
3. Overcoming resistance of trainers to reduce classroom time	• Involve trainers in building new training • Involve trainers in on-the-job coaching • Involve trainers in coaching		
4. Sustaining momentum to keep the project on track	• Build wall charts to track progress publicity • Create a newsletter to inform everyone of changes • Install a process of identifying barriers and escalating problems • Celebrate and publish at key milestones		

Phased-In Approach

Now let's look at this Transition Plan in a little more detail. In the first part of the plan, we plotted out how the individual pieces will be rolled out over a calendar year. You will notice that each phase matches up with the key deliverables of a Learning Path. Measurement starts immediately and continues through the life of the project. As each piece is built, it is phased in.

You'll also notice as you go along that there is a strong need to provide status information and to hold kickoff meetings to introduce new phases. One of the things you will notice in the first plan is that we are launching self-study courses in batches of five. This tends to be a little less messy than adding them one at a time. You might also launch them by logical groups;

for example, everything that is background on the company and the industry could be launched at the same time.

As each self-study reading assignment is placed into service, you need to take the following actions to integrate it:

1. Schedule it in the sequence of training along the current Learning Path. Is this going to be prework for a class or will it be used with on-the-job coaching?

2. Revise classroom portions. If this reading assignment replaces a classroom lecture, you need to make sure that there is a debriefing of the material and some type of practice activity. This also means that you will need to revise your classroom agenda.

3. Build a coaches' guide. If this reading assignment is going to be coordinated with on-the-job coaching, you need to provide instructions on how the coach will debrief the material and arrange live practice.

In the final phase, all of the major development has been finished and tested. This is an excellent time to reenergize the project by holding a roll-out meeting to present current results and show the new training. You've come a long way and everyone has done a lot of good work, so make a big deal out of it.

Motivation and Communication Issues

The second part of the transition plan looks at key motivation and communication issues. It's important to know where the resistance will be coming from and take proactive steps to head it off. Some resistance is natural because you are changing how people do their jobs and taking them out of their comfort zones by moving away from a very traditional approach.

Here are some key ideas for dealing with resistance:

• Hold overview and kickoff sessions.

• Give everyone the big picture of what's going to be happening and, if possible, involve upper management to show that they are supporting this effort.

- Encourage participation in all phases.

- Participation builds ownership. We find that people want to participate and have their ideas included. People tend not to resist their own ideas and work.

- Communicate progress.

- Post results and make sure everyone knows what's next. Using an email newsletter is a good idea.

- Celebrate and reward progress as well as success. Don't wait until the end.

- Make sure these ideas are incorporated into your project plan.

Maintenance Planning

Now that you've successfully launched your Learning Path project and all the training has been built or revised, what's next? As with any training initiative, it's always difficult to sustain momentum, keep things up-to-date, and make improvements. This will have been obvious when you worked on Quick Hits and saw a lot of old and outdated materials.

The first part of your maintenance plan is to establish owners or keepers of the content. This means that someone has to be assigned to make sure that the content is always current and up-to-date. This should be someone who has a stake in making sure everything is correct, as well as someone who will always be close to where the changes are made. This means that every time there is a policy or procedural change, a new marketing program, or a new customer, there is a corresponding change in the training. This needs to happen simultaneously with the change.

There also must be an overall owner or keeper of the Learning Path. That means that, if marketing wants to add training on a new product, it needs to be fit into the Learning Path and follow the learning methodology that has been established. If marketing says they just want to put on a half-day PowerPoint presentation, the keeper of the path has to insist that "We no longer do half-day lectures, and some thought must be given on how this information will be integrated into the job and placed on the Learning Path." Otherwise, you're right back where you started.

Keepers of the content and keepers of the path have to have the support and authority required to maintain the integrity of the training. That's why these people should have a major stake in the training. Process owners and department heads make great keepers of the content. They can get help with the actual work that's involved, but they have to have the final say. Also, this requires that senior leadership delegate the authority to say yes or no to how training is done to learning experts.

If you remember, earlier in this book we talked about using training methods and materials that are easy to build and easy to update. Microsoft Word® documents, PowerPoint presentations, printed job aides, online help, and digital video are all relatively easy to replace. It's important that anyone who is going to do revisions have a proficient skill level in all the technology and software programs. This may require that you add this type of training into their Learning Paths.

Learning Management Systems

Finally, a valuable tool for making maintenance easier is a good learning management system (LMS). Like a lot of software solutions, an LMS is a technology without content. It helps schedule and track training as well as providing ways to test and track results. Most LMSs are designed to hold a curriculum or series of courses. In fact, any self-study materials can be linked or downloaded through the LMS.

We suggest that you upload the Learning Path rather than a curriculum and use it to track new employees' progress through the Learning Path. All of the tests in the self-study can be placed in the LMS, and you can then track individual and class results. There are a lot of learning management systems on the market. As you look for one, try to find one that will be the most compatible with a Learning Path and with housing all of the related materials. The LMS needs to provide real-time data and be easy to update. A robust content management system will streamline maintenance when integrated with your LMS.

Reporting Results

As the leader of a Learning Path Initiative, you will need to report these results on a periodic basic as well as at major milestones. Earlier we showed a sample of the report that is made at the end of the first thirty days. Now that we have people who are completing the revised Learning Path, it is time to report results. For this example of reporting back the results, we will assume we are working on a customer service Learning Path. In this report, we have just put the first group of fifty new employees through the revised Learning Path and measured the results against our baseline measures. A similar report should be made when a reengineered Learning Path has been implemented. Figures 7.1 through 7.7 illustrate the example.

Figure 7.1. Customer Service Learning Path

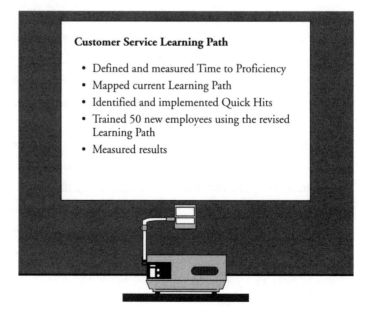

Customer Service Learning Path

- Defined and measured Time to Proficiency
- Mapped current Learning Path
- Identified and implemented Quick Hits
- Trained 50 new employees using the revised Learning Path
- Measured results

Figure 7.1 is a quick review of what has happened to date. It maps to the steps of developing a Learning Path. Figure 7.2 provides the basic measures for reporting results. Using these measures, when the group of fifty new employees is proficient they will handle 1,250 orders per day, yielding $62,500. In this example there was no attrition. If there were any, it would naturally reduce the output. Figure 7.3 shows a quick recap of what happened to the Learning Path to reduce Time to Proficiency.

Figure 7.4 shows the first big results. It shows that in the past it took ninety days to reach proficiency. The new group of fifty became proficient in sixty days. The sales per day as the old and new groups became proficient are shown in Figure 7.5. You'll notice that the new group started taking orders sooner and reached proficiency thirty days earlier. Once they reached proficiency, their performance continued to increase so, even at ninety days, the performance of the two groups was different.

Figure 7.2. Definition of Proficiency

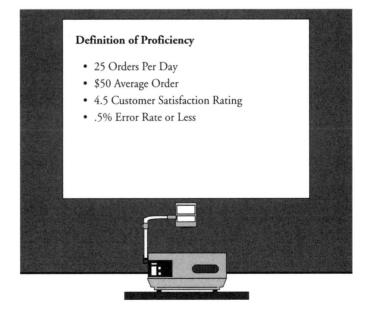

Definition of Proficiency

- 25 Orders Per Day
- $50 Average Order
- 4.5 Customer Satisfaction Rating
- .5% Error Rate or Less

Figure 7.3. Quick Hits

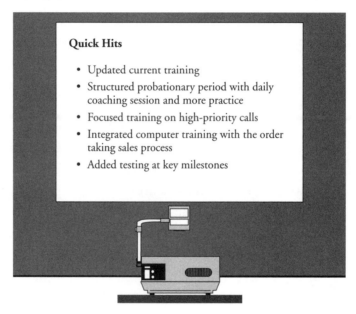

Figure 7.4. Reduction in Time to Proficiency

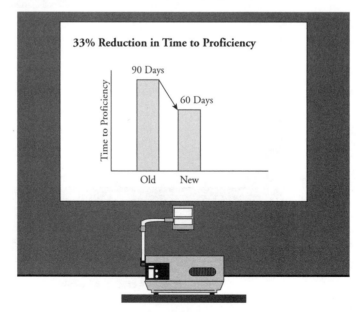

Figure 7.5. Sales Increase

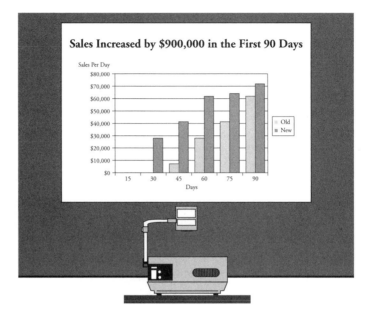

Figure 7.6. Money Saved

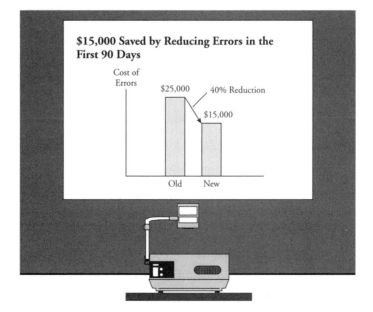

Figure 7.7. Customer Satisfaction

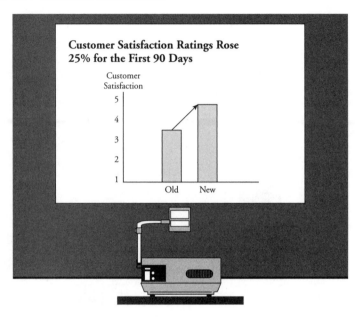

Figure 7.6 translates the difference in the errors made by the two groups into actual dollars. In this example, an error cost about $50 in terms of returns, administration, shipping, and restocking. Figure 7.7 shows the effect of the new Learning Path on customer satisfaction. Again, the new group got to proficiency faster and continued to improve.

Summary

In this chapter we looked at a range of issues and ideas on how to implement and maintain a Learning Path. You'll find that you can't over-communicate with or over-involve stakeholders. This is a major change and there will always be resistance that slows momentum.

To conclude Part I of this book, in the next chapter we will be looking at ideas for the overall management of a Learning Path Initiative. It is not designed to present basic project management but rather to bring out ideas and templates on how to specifically manage this type of training initiative.

8

Managing Learning Path Projects

BUILDING AND IMPLEMENTING Learning Paths, with all the associated training, often becomes a large and sometimes unwieldy project. Therefore, it's important to manage this project with a lot of planning, tracking, and discipline. We've had as many as a dozen or more Learning Paths being built at the same time. Without good structures and systems, these projects can get off track and sometimes grind to a halt.

Common Pitfalls

Before we get into the how-to's of managing this type of project, let's start with a quick list of the reasons why this and other training projects get into deep water. As you try one of these projects, it's always a good idea to come back to this list when you start to have problems. You'll probably see the trouble on this list.

Lack of Support

Building and installing Learning Paths is a major change initiative. Without upper management support, there won't be enough momentum to be able to make the change. The project can also be sabotaged at all levels if upper management is not fully on board.

Lack of Participation

The only way to build support and ownership for a Learning Path is to make sure that all stakeholders are involved in the planning and development. This means making sure that everyone gets involved with reviews and pilot tests. It also means that stakeholders have an opportunity to give their opinions during the research phase.

Lack of Adequate Reviews

This means that not only are the right people involved in reviewing plans, designs, and documents but also that they spend enough time and do a complete job. If this isn't done, you get a lot of pushback during the implementation of the training.

Unclear Role Definitions

People have different roles to play according to their stake in the outcome and their expertise. A subject-matter expert looking for typos is a misuse of time and resources. Also, making sure that training is done right and applies the correct principles lies with the training experts and not the line managers or participants.

Accepting Only Perfection

The building of training is an iterative process. It needs to be okay to make changes as you go. Expecting that every version is perfect and that you only need to pilot test final training is unrealistic and blocks creativity and risk taking. People need to be open-minded through the development process. Don't be defensive, and encourage others to be just as open.

Missing Stakeholders

When you miss stakeholders, you often end up either with a biased view on what needs to be taught or with misaligned priorities. It's important to really look at who will be affected by the outcome of the training and ask them to participate. The most commonly missed stakeholders are customers, and yet they are the ones who are often the most effected by the training.

Lack of Testing

This is linked to the acceptance of perfection only. You never know how something is really going to work unless you test it. Testing can include pilots, but also walkthroughs with key individuals.

Inadequate Resources

The biggest resource issue is usually the lack of people to do the job quickly and at an expert level. Building training requires specific expertise at key points in time. Relying on current staff can put a big strain on their time, and they may not have the full capabilities to do everything. Therefore, it's a good idea to look at ways to outsource some of the design and development of training. Divide the reviews among the content experts for speed and broader participation.

Building Support

Building and continuing to build support for your Learning Path Initiative is crucial. Here are some ideas we have on how to gain and build commitment as you go along. The first and foremost way of building support for Learning Paths is to implement the 30/30 Plan in order to prove that the Learning Path Method works and to demonstrate real business results.

It's critical that, when you select the first function for a Learning Path, the owner of the function strongly supports what you are trying to do. In any organization there are always innovators and early adopters who will recognize the opportunity and potential benefits of a change initiative. In the long run, they will become the advocates and the teachers of the rest of the organization.

It's important that the first sponsors or champions of this Learning Path Methodology have the ear of the business leader and have real credibility with the senior leadership of the company. You will be asking sponsors to put their credibility on the line, but they will see that the risks are small and the returns are huge. It will then be easier to find other sponsors; however, picking influential, well-respected champions early on is critical to long-term success and to driving the Learning Path Methodology across the enterprise.

You will also find many of your strongest supporters in functions that are in trouble or rapidly expanding. Here the business need is the greatest, and there is a lot of urgency around taking action. In particular, anyone involved in business process outsourcing or acquisition integration will have a strong and immediate need for Learning Paths.

The second method of building support is providing opportunities for all key stakeholders to get involved and play an active role. Some of the key guidelines for encouraging involvement include:

- Find an executive sponsor to invite others to be involved.
- Make it clear up-front how much time will be needed for those who volunteer.
- Allow teams to invite others to be involved.
- Require that, once you are involved, you need to commit to staying with it for the entire project.
- Make it easy to be involved up-front so that you can limit new people joining later.
- Expand your research so that everyone is asked to give an opinion, even if you don't use it.
- Give credit to others so that they will accept ownership of the final output.
- Communicate results so that others will want to be involved in future projects.
- Celebrate success early and often. Don't forget to put it in the project plan.

The two groups that will be the biggest challenge to involve in building Learning Paths will be existing trainers and managers who will be asked to be trainers. Since, as you build Learning Paths, you will be moving training from the classroom into self-study and on-the-job training, there will be less work for classroom trainers. It's natural for these trainers to resist working on Learning Paths because they may see it as working themselves out of a job.

While you may be reducing headcount in the training department, you will have a new need to be able to design and write training in new forms, other than traditional workbooks and leader's guides. Some of your existing trainers can learn to do these new tasks, while others may be able to learn how to facilitate problem-solving sessions and become internal consultants. There will be a need for more train-the-trainer and coaching coaches training. Many of these skills can be developed as a result of working on Learning Paths. There may not be an easy answer for this issue, but it's important to recognize it and take action early.

In most enterprises there is a need for a small number of real experts in the learning function. These people will have the change management skills, along with the internal consulting and instructional design skills, to be able to drive improvements to learning methods across the enterprise.

Avoid adding full-time members of the training department just because they are available or show some interest or potential. There will be a lot of work to be done on the Learning Path Teams with part-time involvement from employees across the organization. It is better if they keep their day jobs.

Most of the solution development and writing should be subcontracted to outside experts at competitive rates. A reduced number of dedicated trainers will be able to focus on developing leaders and coaches. The real advantage of using managers as instructors and coaches is the opportunity to develop their skills as leaders and communicators because teaching is leadership.

Development Process

With these ideas about how to build support in mind, let's go on to discuss how to manage a Learning Path Initiative. In managing any training project such as Learning Paths, it's useful to know that most projects follow a three-phase development process, as in Figure 8.1. You will see many different versions of this process, but in essence they are all the same.

Figure 8.1. Three-Phase Development Process

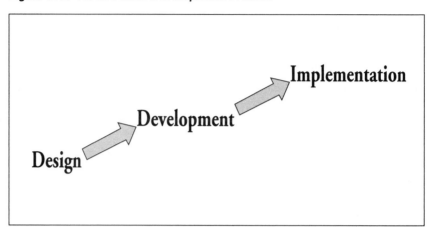

Design

The first part of the process is to create a detailed training design that specifies the learning objectives, content, and activities to be included. To develop the design usually requires some type of research, such as a needs analysis, but as we will discuss in Chapter 12, Capturing Content, a broad range of research activities can be done.

Designs are critical because they allow you to make changes and take new directions before anything is built. It's like having a blueprint for a house before you start to pour the foundation. It's easier to move the rooms around on paper than it would be after the house is built.

We recommend building a course outline for each part of the Learning Path. This is usually sufficient for building a self-study reading assignment. However, a more detailed design will be needed for e-learning and classroom training before you build anything new.

Again, it's critical that you have a broad group of stakeholders provide input and that the design be thoroughly reviewed before anything is developed.

Development

From the design, you are now ready to begin building the training. Often, you won't have enough information from your preliminary research to actually build the program. You should plan to go back and get the details on a second round of research.

Just like design, development is an iterative process. That means you are highly unlikely to reach perfection on the first draft. We prefer to write a first draft, get feedback, make revisions, and then go on to some type of pilot test. Later in this chapter we'll talk more about pilot tests as well as reviews. At the end of the development stage you should have a completed and approved training program ready for implementation.

Implementation

Implementation is the phase where the training is rolled out to the larger audience. It starts with some type of production, either printing materials, loading files on a website, or finishing production of a video and putting it on CDs.

Implementation includes scheduling as well as tracking the results of the training and making any changes. There is also ongoing maintenance of the training to make sure it's up-to-date and correct.

Implementation also includes anything you intend to do to increase compliance as well as reward or certify results.

Again, the purpose of looking at this development process is to provide a framework for how we will be planning out and tracking our Learning Paths and all of the associated training projects.

Organization

Organization is all about having the right people in the right roles in order to make this large-sized project run smoothly. It's usually a good idea to get one function completed to have the experience of how to do Learning Paths before rolling it out across the organization. This also has the advantage of creating Learning Path experts who can tutor or coach other functions.

The first step is to assemble a steering committee or master Learning Path Team responsible for:

- Selecting which function to do and in what order

- Making sure that all work is consistent and follows the methodology and format

- Providing support and escalating issues when progress stalls

- Training functional teams on Learning Paths

- Managing and forecasting the overall budgets and training plans

The steering committee should include the following individuals:

- Senior training manager

- Senior executive or business leader sponsor of the initiative

- Senior quality manager (to lead the measurement part of this project)

- Internal or external training consultants, writers, and developers

- Subject-matter experts (SMEs)

- Any other volunteers from the executive leadership or process owners

The titles and jobs of all these people will vary from organization to organization. What's important is to have a high level of support from senior leadership as well as training expertise. This team won't need to meet very often once all the functional teams are up and running.

On a functional level, there needs to be a work team to map out the Learning Path for that function as well as build any required training. This is a blend of operational experts, managers, top performers, and training staffs. It's critical that there be a champion or owner of this function who has a commitment to getting the Learning Path in place. In selecting where to start building Learning Paths, this is a critical decision.

What's usually missing in most organizations is the expertise to design and develop training. Specifically, when it gets down to writing training, there may not be anyone on staff who can do an adequate job. This is because most companies haven't had large training or human resources departments for over twenty years. Most of that work is outsourced.

The good news is that there are a lot of outside contractors who can do this type of work. You only need to use them when you are ready and only pay them for the work they do. Adding these vendors to the teams, on an as-needed basis, is an excellent idea.

In many cases, a lot of this work can be done by teleconference, email, or online services like Webex. Since you are mostly moving around documents and talking about them, there is often little need to meet in person. This expands your pool of vendors to anyone with a phone and a computer.

Building Learning Paths involves the coordinated effort of experts from different disciplines. If you try to have one person do everything, it won't work. Even if you have enough people who all have the same skill set, it won't work.

At some point you will need writers and you will need a lot of them for a limited period of time. There are two reasons to use vendors. The first is to meet the surge of demands and the second is to use experts. People who write for a living will be able to produce usable materials fast. They will be able to pick up the Learning Path Methodology quickly from this book. You can put them on a short Learning Path to get them up-to-speed on your project.

Use the same thought process to bring in other experts. Tap into what they do best. This is true for subject-matter experts, media/e-learning designers, instructors, senior management/champions, coaches, guides, facilitators, and quality/measurement experts. Think about a Learning Path for your project and how to bring in these experts just in time. Putting them on a Learning Path will go a long way toward demonstrating what we are doing here.

Planning and Tracking

A major challenge of trying to manage a large training project is being able to manage a large number of pieces and parts through the development process. If you are working with ten Learning Paths at the same time, that's a lot of activity, especially if you're creating ten to thirty self-study reading assignments and revised classroom training as well.

Planning helps determine how much you can actually accomplish, how long it will take, and whether you have enough people working on the project. While you can usually get a current Learning Path in place within two weeks because you are only working with what currently exists, you may also assemble ten paths in two weeks if you have ten teams working on them. Keep in mind that if you are going to review all those paths, you can't do them all in one day.

Now consider that you are going to build ten self-study reading assignments for each of ten Learning Paths. That's one hundred self-study courses. Assume that it takes one week to write, review, and edit each course. If you have one writer working on all of them it would take one hundred weeks or just about two years. Not very timely, is it? If you have ten writers, it would only take ten weeks. However, now you have the issue of making sure the work is consistent among the ten writers and that all the simultaneous work is done, too.

We've found that the easiest part of doing this type of work quickly is to add writers. However, what tends to happen is that they produce large volumes of work that have to be reviewed. If it takes a day to review each self-study reading assignment, one person can't do all the reviews. It just takes too long and bogs down the process.

To help you with this type of project management, we've provided planning and tracking templates (Exhibits 8.1 through 8.5) to help you with building both Learning Paths and self-study reading assignments. The first tool is the Learning Path Project Plan in Exhibit 8.1. It provides you with all of the major steps. You need to decide how you will do each step. Assign duties and set deadlines. For example, if there is a line item for conducting research, you can then add into the "How" column how you will be doing that research, for example, with interviews and focus groups.

At the bottom of the plan, you'll notice that we've added some color codes. We find that this is particularly helpful for identifying items that need immediate attention. Just by looking at the colors you can tell at a glance if a project is on track.

The second template is the Learning Path Tracking Sheet in Exhibit 8.2. This is used to track the progress of multiple Learning Paths as they are developed. In the first column, write in all of the Learning Paths in progress. Then put a date under each item when it's completed. Again, the color codes will tell you which Learning Paths are on track and which ones are in trouble.

Exhibit 8.1. Learning Path Project Plan

Job or Function: _____   Today's Date: _____   Estimated Completion Date: _____

Steps	How	How	Due	Done
1. Identify and recruit team members				
2. Hold team kickoff planning meeting				
3. Develop research plan				
4. Conduct research				
5. Develop and present research report				
6. Develop baseline measures				
7. Gather baseline data				
8. Map current Learning Path				
9. Validate Learning Path				
10. Identify Quick Hits				
11. Create plan for implementing Quick Hits				
12. Build a proficiency model				
13. Align proficiency model to business needs				
14. Determine how to accelerate the Learning Path				
15. Build required training				
16. Revise Learning Path with new training				
17. Measure results				
18. Create maintenance plan				

Red = Alert needs immediate attention Yellow = Delayed or behind schedule Green = On track

Exhibit 8.2. Learning Path Tracking Sheet

Functions	Select Team Members	Kickoff	Define Time to Proficiency	Map Learning Path	Quick Hits	Acceleration	New Learning Path	Transition	Maintenance	Comments

Red = Alert needs immediate attention Yellow = Delayed or behind schedule Green = On track

The next two templates are used for planning and tracking self-study reading assignments. Exhibit 8.3, the Self-Study Project Plan, helps track individual courses for a function through all of the stages of development. Again, write in the dates that each part was completed.

The template in Exhibit 8.4 helps you track the progress of Self-Study training that is being developed for multiple paths. This will be particularly useful for looking at resources and budgets required.

Now let's talk about some of the related issues in project management. These include how to do reviews, edit and proof, run pilot tests, and train Learning Path Teams.

Reviews

Reviews by subject-matter experts and stakeholders are critical to make sure that the content of any training is correct. However, this is often the point at which training projects grind to a halt. It takes a lot of time to review a one-hundred-page document, especially if you've never been trained on how to do this type of review. In addition, as we mentioned earlier, if a document needs to go to a legal department, you may never see it again. However, you can't skip critical reviews.

Here are some tips on how to get reviews done in a quick and meaningful fashion:

Establish a Review Committee

A review committee consists of subject-matter experts, stakeholders, and end users. A review committee should have three to ten members. The review committee needs to include anyone who has final signoff on the document. Review committee members need to commit to the project from start to end. No one should be added to the committee once the project starts. Adding new members as you go along is a great way to torpedo this type of project. They will try to insert their own ideas and agendas into what has already been done and agreed to. You will also have to spend a lot of time getting these new people up-to-speed. You need to establish how much time you expect from review committee members and make sure they understand their roles and obligations.

Exhibit 8.3. Self-Study Project Plan

Job or Function: _____ Today's Date: _____ Estimated Completion Date: _____

Course	Outline	Review	Research	Review	First Draft	Review	Revisions	Review	Edit and Proof	Production	Comments

Red = Alert needs immediate attention Yellow = Delayed or behind schedule Green = On track

Exhibit 8.4. Self-Study Tracking Sheet

Function	# of Course	Outline	Research	First Draft	Revisions	Edit and Proof	Production	Comments

Red = Alert needs immediate attention   Yellow = Delayed or behind schedule   Green = On track

Focus on Content

The review committee is there to make sure you are teaching the right stuff. The members are not experts in instructional design and you don't want them changing the learning methodology or formats. In addition, you want to make sure that they don't get hung up on typos and grammatical errors. As they review any document, they only need to answer the following questions:

- Is the content complete?

- Is the content correct and current?

- Is the content in the right sequence?

- Are there additional sources of content that should be used?

Establish a Review Cycle

There has to be a review of the design of every document and then another after each draft. There doesn't need to be a full review of a final draft because usually all that was done was a final proof. Plan for about a half day to review each draft of a one-hundred-page document.

Reserve Meetings for Discussion and Brainstorming

Meetings can take up a lot of time. It's not a very good use of time to go through a document page by page if members of the review committee haven't reviewed the document in detail first. Sometimes, the only formal meeting you really need to have is an early design meeting to set out the structure of the training.

Capture Changes and Comments in Writing

Have each member of the review committee make his or her changes and comments on the document and then send a copy to you. You can then make one master document that combines all of the changes and suggestions. This can be circulated back to the review committee. If there is a lot of disagreement, then it's useful to have either a teleconference or a review committee meeting. Otherwise, the written comments are sufficient.

Pilot Tests

We like to use pilot tests anytime there will be new or revised training. This will be true for installing a new Learning Path, new self-study, or new classroom materials. No matter how good instructional designers are, there are always a lot of surprises when you see how participants react and respond to training.

One of the big mistakes we see when pilots are used is that they don't go into a pilot stage early enough in the development process. They won't go into a pilot until everything is done and as perfect as possible. At this point the investment in time and money is so high that you can't afford to make any major changes, even if the training is off-track. This is especially true if any video or e-learning has been fully produced.

Also, by going to pilots earlier, you can shorten the review cycle because the pilot serves as a review by end users. This is often far more useful than sitting around a conference table reviewing documents page by page.

Editing and Proofing

While you are building and accelerating Learning Paths and all the associated training, you will be generating a large number of documents. At some point in time, all of these documents need to be edited and proofed. Here are some quick tips on how to make this part of the project run smoothly:

Make It the Last Step

A lot of time is wasted on editing and proofing documents before they are in a final stage. There are few things more worthless than proofing pages that end up in the wastebasket after a review cycle. Everyone involved needs to be able to accept that a rough draft or even first draft is rough and will have a few typos and grammatical errors. Everything will get cleaned up on the final drafts.

Use Format and Style Templates

It takes a lot of time to clean up documents that are written with different formats, styles, and tones of voice. It's critical that both the writers and editors work from a template and that they stick to it. This may require some training in how to use basic programs like Microsoft Word, PowerPoint, or Excel. Even making decisions such as how many spaces between sentences or how to use commas can save a lot of editing time.

Insist on Spell-Checking Documents

No document should be passed along without a final run through a spell checking program. Even a long document only takes a minute or two to check. If documents aren't checked, it's a sign that the writer may not know how to use that part of their program.

Outsource When Possible

Let's assume that you are going to write twenty-five new, self-study reading assignments for a Learning Path. That's a lot of proofing. If one person does all the proofing it might take you four to six weeks to get all that proofing done. If that proofing is being done by a staff person who has other duties, it will take a lot longer. It's better to outsource this proofing to a firm that can dedicate five or six editors to your project. Editing help is usually not very expensive and is easy to find. Every city has a number of secretarial services that can do this type of work. This is better than hiring temps because of the uneven flow of documents to be proofed. They don't come all at once. They tend to come in batches.

Training for Learning Path Teams

As you've probably gathered as you've read through this book, there is a considerable amount of knowledge and skills required to build and implement Learning Paths. A lot of what needs to be learned is also very new or a shift away from what has been done in the past.

What we've always done to address this issue is to create a Learning Path for working on this type of project. Along with the Learning Path, we created a series of self-study reading assignments and mapped out all of the on-the-job learning required. We also developed coaches who could guide others through the training. The result was that it worked very well and the teams got up-to-speed quickly. They also were able to experience a Learning Path first-hand.

It should be pointed out that some skills take a long time to develop and, if they are not present in your workforce, the best idea is usually to contract out that work. In particular, there is a lot of training design and writing. These are skills that are not mastered through a single training course and often take years of practical experience. Writers will tell you that the only way they develop and maintain their skill is by writing every day.

Virtual Teams

A general Learning Path form you can use is on the following page (Exhibit 8.5). We've added a series of columns on the right. In these columns, write in the names of the individuals you plan to develop. Then customize the path for each participant by placing an X next to each line item you want the person to complete.

Notice how there is a self-study course combined with practical experience for each line item. They need to include additional information other than what's included in this book. For example, there is a lot more to conducting training research than we can include in this book. In addition to the ones listed, you may want to add some other skill training, such as:

- Facilitating Meetings
- Quality Measurement
- Instructional Design
- Business Writing
- Presentation Skills
- Project Management
- Planning
- Budgeting

Exhibit 8.5. Learning Path for Teams

Day	What	How	1	2	3	4	5
	Learning Paths Overview	• Read the book, kickoff meeting					
	Conducting Research	Conducting Research Self-Study • Write 1 research plan • Conduct 5 interviews • Conduct 2 focus groups • Write and present a research report					
	Measurement	Measurement Self-Study • Work with a quality expert on establishing baseline measures • Establish baseline measures for a function					
	Map a Current Learning Path	Mapping a Learning Path Self-Study • Work with a quality expert on establishing baseline measures • Establish baseline measures for a function					
	Finding Quick Hits	Finding Quick Hits Self-Study • Participate on a team looking for Quick Hits • Facilitate a Finding Quick Hits session					
	Coaching	Coaching Self-Study • Observe a coach working with new employees • Coach 2 new employees					
	Accelerating a Learning Path	Acceleration Self-Study • Participate on a team looking for ways to accelerate Learning Path • Facilitate an acceleration session					
	Project Management	Project Management Self-Study • Participate on a Learning Path Team • Lead a Learning Path Team					
	Conducting Reviews	Review Self-Study • Review 2 Learning Paths • Review 5 self-study reading assignments					

Summary

In summary, managing a Learning Path project is very similar to managing any other type of training initiative. It's critical to do the planning and tracking required and to train others on the Learning Path Methodology. Periodically, it's a good idea to look at the reasons we presented for why projects get in trouble to see if you are headed for any trouble as you go along.

Part II

Doing the "Right Training"

PART II CONSISTS of four chapters that focus on making sure that what is included in the Learning Path connects with the business and is current, complete, and accurate. Each chapter is designed to add depth and direction to the Learning Path Methodology presented in Part I. While there are many more techniques that can be used in this area, these are the ones we feel are the most important and work the best. Here is a brief summary of what you will be reading about in each chapter.

Chapter 9: Building Proficiency Models

Chapter 9 is focused on how to connect a Learning Path to the combination of skills, knowledge, and attitudes that are required to perform a task or function. This chapter introduces the concept of a proficiency model and contrasts it to traditional competency models.

Chapter 10: Developing Top Performers

Chapter 10 looks at how to use Learning Paths to train and develop anyone in any function in an organization. It looks at what happens after new employees become independent and are ready to move to the next level. It also looks at how to build Learning Paths for functions that have only one or two employees.

Chapter 11: Connecting to Business Needs

While Chapters 9 and 10 are focused on ways to make sure a job is done the right way, in this chapter we look at what to do as the organization changes and moves in new directions. This chapter shows how to use Learning Paths during strategic planning and other business planning within the organization. Using Learning Paths in this way allows an organization's learning leaders to be proactive or strategic partners, rather than just a support function.

Chapter 12: Capturing Content

In Chapter 12 we look at strategies for capturing what the organization knows and knows how to do. Throughout this book we stress the importance of writing things down and making content king. This chapter shows you how.

9

Building Proficiency Models

BUILDING A PROFICIENCY MODEL is the first step in making sure we are doing the right training. When we first started working on Learning Paths, we used to insist on building a competency model as a way of verifying that we were teaching the right stuff. However, competency models can be difficult or confusing to build, and they are often not specific enough to be really valuable. So we turned to building a proficiency model, which linked much better to our concept of Time to Proficiency.

To better understand this concept and learn how to build a proficiency model, let's go back and look at competency models first to lay down a good foundation for where we are headed. Besides, the underlying concept of a competency model still has a lot of value.

A fairly generic definition of a competency model is the knowledge, skills, or attitude required to perform a task or function. Sometimes you will see the word "attribute" substituted for "attitude." Here is a quick description of each.

Knowledge

Knowledge is the cognitive domain. This is basically *what you can remember, interpret, apply, or comprehend.* Here are some examples of what you might know about geography:

- Recite the names of the capitals of European countries.

- Point out the location of Brazil on a map.

- Explain why it's hot in Ecuador and cold in Calgary.

Note how each of these examples includes an action verb that describes what an individual can do with this knowledge. Contrast this with phrases such as the "currency of Mexico" or the "population of Minneapolis."

"Peso" and "365,000" are simply facts. These are not descriptive of why the knowledge is required. Better requests might be

- Distinguish pesos from dollars and francs.

- Differentiate between the size of the population in Minneapolis as compared to Denver or Chicago.

Often when teams brainstorm knowledge competencies they end up with the topic headlines from training courses. These are often categories of knowledge that don't really relate to how that knowledge is used. It's difficult, but we always try to push back on this work and insist that teams use action verbs and think about how the knowledge is actually used.

Skills

Skills are the behavioral or psychomotor domain. A skill is *a behavior or set of behaviors.* For example, serving a tennis ball and driving a car are skills. Here are some business-related skills:

- Write a proposal.

- Facilitate a meeting.

- Give a speech.

- Demonstrate empathy.

- Build support and consensus.

- Adapt to personality styles.
- Conduct a problem-solving session.
- Analyze a problem.
- Create a process map.
- Document a call.
- Search for a name.
- Create a database.

One of the challenges in writing competencies is to separate knowledge from skills. For example, there is a difference between knowing how to document a call and actually doing it. In many cases, skills involve being able to put what you know into action. We'll try to make this easier to do as we move on to proficiencies.

Attitudes

Attitudes are *the affective or emotional domain.* We know that the way we look at or react to different situations has an effect on our performance. You will do your job differently if you believe that customers are valuable and you need to do everything to keep them, versus if you believe that customers are really stupid and they make a lot of extra work for you. In addition, for new employees to be productive, they need to be able to share the values and norms of the organization.

You will also find that top performers tend to share a common set of attitudes or beliefs about their jobs. Top salespeople like and are invigorated by meeting new people, while others are reluctant or even fearful.

Competency Models

A competency model groups, arranges, and prioritizes competencies in a logical and usable way. To build a competency model we like to use the same method we use with most documents and models. We get a team together to get something down on paper and then we get stakeholders and experts to make their additions and changes. This reduces the amount of time spent working on the obvious and focuses everyone's time on expanding on or correcting what is known.

We often use two different approaches to building a competency model, depending on what we already know about a function. One method involves brainstorming all of the knowledge, skills, and attitudes for a position and then determining how to group and arrange them. Each group is given a name or a label. For example, "write a proposal," "facilitate a meeting," and "give a speech" could all fall into the category of communication skills. "Conduct a problem-solving session," "analyze a problem," and "create a process map" might group together under research skills or perhaps planning skills.

We can also do this process in reverse. Take sales, for example; we know that most competencies will fall into the areas of prospecting, goal setting and planning, building relationships, making sales presentations, managing accounts, and product knowledge.

You certainly could add to or modify this list quickly to cover the world of sales. What the competency team would do is brainstorm the competencies within these categories. Product knowledge might include industry knowledge, company knowledge, and competitive knowledge. As you figure out how this knowledge is actually used, you can improve the way the competencies are written.

Using either method, you will end up with a rough draft of a competency model that is about 90 percent accurate. You can probably get to this point in a few hours. Circulating this model for review with stakeholders and experts will get you close to a valid and accurate competency model. Since we are going to be using this model for training purposes and not hiring purposes, this is probably sufficient without doing more advanced surveys and studies.

Proficiency Models

So now we are going to turn this competency model into a proficiency model. The problem with a competency model is that, on the job, we seldom use knowledge, skills, and attitudes in isolation. We use them in combinations and often simultaneously. Simply put, it's not enough to know how to chew gum and how to walk. What you really need to be able to do is chew gum and walk at the same time.

Another example would be what is involved in working in a customer service call center. You need to be talking with a customer in a friendly, upbeat manner. You need to be able to solve problems using a logical, problem-solving process. Plus, you need to be able to look up information and document the call in your computer system. However, you could be able to do all of these competencies individually but not be able to do them at the same time. In this environment, being able to use the phone and your computer at the same time is critical. By identifying these connections, we can then build training that focuses on this type of multi-tasking, rather than teaching everything topic by topic.

Few competency models focus on the level or degree of competence involved. There is seldom a reference to speed, volume, accuracy, or quality. Take a competency such as being able to write a sales proposal. This doesn't have any indication about whether the sales proposal would meet your standards or actually win any business. It also doesn't tell you whether the proposal takes a day, a month, a week, or a year to write.

To get to a proficiency from this competency takes a lot of thought and analysis. We need to ask the question, "What do you really mean by 'write a proposal'?" Some additional questions that would help this analysis include:

- Who is the audience for this proposal?

- Are we responding to Requests for Proposals or not?

- How many proposals do we need to write in a week?

- Are there some specific writing skills or level of accuracy required?

- Does this proposal need to be pre-tested or approved?

- Does the proposal need to be created or entered in any specific software?

- Does the proposal need to use or follow a proposal format or a template?

Depending on the answers to these questions, a proficiency might look like one of the following:

- Respond in writing to customer requests for proposals using the form and providing the information requested by the customer within seven days of a customer request.

- Create a dynamic PowerPoint sales proposal using multimedia to demonstrate our capabilities.

- Build a proposal that demonstrates a strong business case for using our products versus the competition's.

Let's take another example. You'll often see "facilitate a meeting" as a competency. This is a fairly generic skill, but facilitating a quality team meeting is a lot different from facilitating a strategic planning session for an executive group. Here are some examples of proficiencies you might be looking for:

- Facilitate executive level, problem-solving sessions that will lead to consensus and a plan of action.

- Facilitate weekly quality team meetings, making sure that team norms, standards, and processes are followed.

- Facilitate weekly training meetings that provide skill practice for new employees.

In many jobs, we find that there are one or maybe two proficiencies that will have a big effect on whether or not an employee will stay in a job long-term. Here are some quick examples of what we mean:

- *Collector:* Being willing to call strangers at home and ask them to pay what they owe

- *Salesperson:* Being willing to cold call potential prospects to set up appointments to make a sales pitch

- *Factory Worker:* Being willing to work eight hours a day wearing full safety gear, including ear plugs and safety glasses

- *Customer Service Rep:* Being able to greet each and every customer, day in and day out, with a high level of enthusiasm

By going through the process of building a proficiency model, you will develop a very good guide for what it really takes to do a job. You'll also be able to explain the job better to prospective and new employees.

Now what do you do with this proficiency model? The first thing is to go through the list and determine whether a new employee is expected to bring this proficiency to the job or whether it will be part of his or her new-hire training. If you expect all new employees to have a lot of experience building spreadsheets in Excel, this doesn't need to be in the new-hire training.

Next you need to cross-reference your Learning Path to the proficiency model. The best time to do this is after the Quick Hit step and before the acceleration step. This is because in the Quick Hit step, you are only looking for ways to shorten the path.

As you review your Learning Path, ask the following questions:

- Are we developing all the required proficiencies?

- Is the Learning Path structured so that we are teaching everything in the right combinations and sequences (simple to complex)?

- Are we allotting training time in a way that matches the priorities of the job?

- Are we teaching anything that is irrelevant?

In many cases, you will find that the proficiency model will help you reorganize and streamline your Learning Paths. You are going from something that has been assembled piecemeal over time to something that better relates to the job.

Finally, what you've created is a proficiency model that fits with the job today. It's almost certain that the job will change over time. Often, it changes as the business goes in new directions. Therefore, after you've looked at aligning business needs to training, you will want to come back to the proficiency model and make sure that it reflects future needs as well.

Learning Objectives and Activities

When the time comes to actually build or revise existing training, proficiencies become a natural guide for writing learning objectives. There are usually one or more learning objectives that will lead up to a proficiency. For example, for salespeople who do proposals we showed the competency of "Create a dynamic PowerPoint sales proposal using multimedia to demonstrate our capabilities."

Learning objectives for that competence could include that "As a result of the training salespeople will be able to build a PowerPoint presentation using the animation features; set up and operate a PowerPoint presentation using a projector; and describe our capabilities and answer customer questions.

Then as we look at building activities to accomplish these objectives using a Learning Path approach, we'd start to look at ways to teach one or more of these objectives at the same time and to build in sufficient practice and experience. Many of the best activities are going to involve building and practicing PowerPoint presentations with other members of the sales team and with the sales manager as a coach.

While this example is fairly simple, it does illustrate the process of going from proficiencies to learning objectives to learning activities. And as you can see, our first choice for activities is to try to simulate and then practice the entire set of tasks involved.

Research Resources

Before we leave the topic of proficiencies, to really understand what's happening on a job or what's required you may need to do some additional research. Exhibit 9.1 is a quick checklist of places to find information about proficiencies.

Exhibit 9.1. Research Resources

	Resources for Proficiency Information
1.	Job descriptions
2.	Hiring profiles
3.	Training manuals
4.	Web courses
5.	Course catalogs
6.	Interview notes
7.	Focus group notes
8.	Business goals and strategies
9.	Direct observation
10.	Job aides
11.	Procedure manuals
12.	Existing competency models
13.	Competency models of related functions
14.	Industry publications and training programs
15.	Surveys

Summary

Proficiency models are important for making sure that a Learning Path connects to the way a job is actually performed. Proficiency models are used to overcome the shortcomings of traditional competency models by looking at the combinations and links among skills, knowledge, and attitudes. Today most jobs require a great deal of multi-tasking. When these tasks are taught individually it takes a long time, if ever, for employees to learn to use them at the same time.

Keep in mind that in this discussion of competency and proficiency models we are focusing on how to make training more relevant to the actual job. We are not talking about using a proficiency model for hiring and promotions without the required validation and compliance process.

In the Learning Path Methodology the best time to create a proficiency model is immediately after the 30/30 Plan is built and implemented. It is a good first step for reengineering a Learning Path because it provides a great deal of information on how to resequence and combine learning activities.

10

Developing Top Performers

SO FAR IN THIS BOOK we've focused heavily on getting new employees up-to-speed quickly. We chose that focus because of the numbers of employees who need to be trained and the risk of having untrained employees working with customers. But we could as easily apply the concept of Learning Paths to the larger pool of current employees.

Let's break it down even further. Within the group of current employees you have

- Average performers you want to turn into top performers

- Employees who have been around for a while who are below average performers

- New employees who were hired with a lot of experience and may be Independently Productive soon after their first day

- Employees who have mastered a position and are ready to move up

We also want to talk about those functions that have only a small number of employees, or even just one. This would cover many small and mid-sized businesses that don't have a lot of employees. For this we want to share some of our successes using one-person Learning Paths.

Top Performers

If, on a scale of 1 to 5 (1 = low and 5 = high), average performers rate a 3, somewhere in your workforce you have some 5's who probably do the bulk of the work and produce the majority of the revenue. There has to be something that these top performers know or are able to do that makes them different from average performers. If we can find out what this is, we can put it on a Learning Path to help average performers develop into top performers.

The first step is to repeat some of the research we did when we built the initial Learning Path. In that path, we looked at what an employee needed to know and be able to do to become Independently Productive and meet average performance standards.

So if an average salesperson generates $250,000 per year, we looked at the proficiencies for achieving that level of performance. However, if the top performer is bringing in $1,000,000 per year, that salesperson may be doing the same things better, faster, or using more advanced methods and techniques.

In a sales position, you can often reach the level of average performer by handling basic transactions or a larger volume of small sales. This requires a lower level of sales skills and is often driven by marketing and advertising. At a higher level of sales, the game changes. It requires calling on larger customers and making bigger sales. To do this, one's interpersonal and communications skills need to be better, but also there are sales strategies and planning processes that are different and more advanced. And there is a greater depth of understanding of the products and how they work.

Take, for example, the difference between an average and a high-performing realtor. You might see a number of things:

- Top performers sell more expensive houses.
- Top performers generate more listings and for more expensive houses.

- Top performers have a loyal clientele that refers business.

- Top performers have a greater understanding of all of the issues of buying a house.

- Top performers know more about financing options and how to help buyers through that process.

Have you ever noticed that the best salespeople you meet really know what they're talking about and can get you excited about it? That depth of knowledge doesn't just happen. It takes training and a lot of experience.

So we go through the process of interviews and focus groups with top performers. We also do job shadowing and talk with sales managers and customers. Basically, we ask the following questions:

- Who are your top performers?

- What do top performers do when you observe them?

- How long does it take to go from being an average performer to being a top performer?

- What training is available for a salesperson after new-hire training?

- What experiences do salespeople need to move to the next level?

You will also find that there is a lot of valuable information in performance appraisal forms, developmental plans, and yearly objective-setting sessions. A lot of this information is known, but sometimes not written down.

You also need to separate out those things that are training and non-training issues. An entire range of motivational issues shouldn't be confused with training issues. For example, with salespeople a lot of performance, both good and bad, is driven by compensation. Compensation can easily drive a lot of bad habits, discourage salespeople, or lead to undesired results. In a situation where compensation is based on sales volume instead of profitability, salespeople will often generate a lot of unprofitable sales.

The simple test to identify training issues is to determine whether the employee has performed the task to a desired level in the past. If someone takes fifty calls a day for six months and then drops to thirty-five calls a day, it's unlikely that it's a training issue.

To get to a top performer's Learning Path, we need to do some research and map out the training and experience that top performers have that average performers don't have. Use exactly the same process:

1. Map out all of the existing training.

2. Add in the field experience required, key people they have met, and things they have done.

3. Add any special projects or participation on projects.

4. Validate the path.

5. Look for Quick Hits.

6. Finalize and implement the path.

In many cases, this level of a Learning Path is an ongoing developmental path that may last as long as the employee is in the job. Along with a performance appraisal, you can check on where an employee is on a Learning Path and set goals for completing it or add items to the path.

Below Average Performers

The next group includes existing employees who really are not Independently Productive but who have been around for a while. If you have hired someone who is capable of doing the job, there is usually something missing or incorrect in his or her training. Remember that the person went through a more traditional approach to training where something may have been missed or wasn't taught in a way that sticks.

For these employees, sit down with them and the new employee Learning Path and try to find the missing training. First, go through the Learning Path and identify anything that the employee missed or that has changed since he or she went through training. Schedule that training for completion in the order it appears. The person can go through classroom pieces with the next group of new employees.

You're also going to find that the person missed a lot of the practice, coaching, and experience that is listed on the Learning Path. Assign these employees to a coach and make sure they get what they missed. Focus especially on the missing supervised practice.

Experienced New Hires

At times you are going to hire some very experienced employees. It will be a waste of time to put them through the entire new-hire training program. For these people you can use the same process that we suggested for below average performers. Go through the existing Learning Path and identify what they've missed. You can also develop a method that allows them to test out of any training.

Even with a lot of experience, these people won't have the exact experience with your organization. Therefore, you want to make sure they don't skip any of the coaching and practice described in the Learning Path. This will help them pick up what they need to know on the job. However, be cautious of letting them do things the way they did them in the old company if it's not identical to yours. This creates a lot of variation in processes that makes improvement difficult.

Ready for the Next Level

Good employees are always ready to move up. This will be a lot easier if you've developed a Learning Path for the next level. Start this employee on the Learning Path for the next level. However, you can space this learning over time to coincide with openings at the next level. In this case, the Learning Path and the developmental plan become the same.

Functions with Few Employees

A lot of companies have functions that are done by one or two people. There isn't a formal training program because it doesn't make sense to build and run formal training for one person. Often, the same function has been done by the same person for years, so there's the risk that if that person ever leaves or is promoted, no one will know or be able to do the job.

What we've done in these cases is try to document how this job is done and then create a Learning Path that follows the job process. On this Learning Path, there will be some training that is the same as other functions. Some of the product and computer system training will fall into that category. The rest needs to be in the form of on-the-job coaching that follows the process and steps of that job. We find it is a good idea to capture or write down as much of this as possible.

The big difference with this Learning Path is that you won't be building any new training. Almost everything will be on the job. One thing you can do with the Learning Paths of these small functions is cross-train others so that they can take over in an emergency or if the person is promoted.

You will find that there are a number of other applications for Learning Paths besides just for new employees. If you follow the methodologies in this book, you will find that they easily apply and produce significant results.

Manager/Leadership Paths

Another application of this type of Learning Path is to create a path for ongoing leadership development. This is a long-term track to build management and leadership skills. Again, it needs to be more than just a list of training programs. You must include project and work experience.

To build a leadership/manager path, you need to work on a proficiency model for leaders and managers in your organization. You will also look at the priorities and sequence of those proficiencies. Let's take a look at two proficiencies and see how they translated into a Learning Path.

The first proficiency is "being able to lead and manage a project that meets its goals within time and budget targets." For this version of a Learning Path, we are going to assume that:

- It is designed for one manager at a time. In other words, managers can go through it at any time without waiting for a class to start.

- Generic project management courses are already being taught, both within the organization and at a local college.

- Typical projects that managers will be involved with are shorter term, problem-solving projects initiated by senior management.

As you can see in the leadership path shown in Exhibit 10.1, the new manager first works on an existing project to see how a project is done and then leads a project while learning various project management techniques. This path could also be sequenced so that the new manager works first with simple projects and then later is given increasingly more difficult assignments. You'll also notice the frequent interaction with this new manager's manager to ensure that there is a lot of evaluation, feedback, and coaching.

Exhibit 10.1. Leadership Learning Path 1

Function: Leadership – Project Management   *Date:* Today

Weeks	What	How	Materials	Done
1	• Meet with your manager to discuss Learning Path and expectations	30-Minute Meeting		
2 - 6	• Participate as a team member on a current project • Observe and take notes on how the project was managed and how the team addressed obstacles and barriers	30-Minute Meeting		
7	• Write up a summary report of this project experience • Discuss with manager	On the Job 1-Hour Manager Meeting		
8	• Attend project management basics course	Classroom		
9	• Get project assignment • Develop preliminary project plan	Manager Meeting		
10	• Assemble project team • Team dynamics self-study	On the Job Self-Study		
11	• Hold project kickoff meeting • Meetings management self-study	On the Job Self-Study		
12 - 16	• Lead project • Problem-solving self-study	On the Job Self-Study		
17	• Write up final report • Present to manager • Assess results and repeat steps as required	On the Job Meeting		

Let's take a second example, shown in Exhibit 10.2. Leaders need to be able to coach and provide feedback in order to develop their employees. In this example, we are going to take ten new managers through a two-week Learning Path. We will have two self-study reading assignments that will serve as prework for two classroom discussions and practice sessions. Between sessions, managers will be trying to apply what they have learned.

Exhibit 10.2. Leadership Learning Path 2

Function: Leadership – Coaching   *Date:* Today

Day	What	How	Materials	Done
1	• Coaching self-study - Introduction to coaching - Role of a coach - Assessing performance problems	Self-Study		
2	• Attend Coaching Basics 1 Workshop - Discuss coaching principles and roles - Practice assessing performance problems	Classroom		
3 - 7	• Observe and assess performance problems • Keep a journal	On the Job		
8	• Conduct a coaching session self-study	Self-Study		
9	• Attend Coaching Basics 2 Workshop - Review journals - Coaching process - Practice	Classroom		
10 - 14	• Practice and feedback (observation of participants while they are coaching)	On the Job		
15	• Final debriefing	Classroom		

As you assemble the complete leadership path, you may see some duplication or ways to simplify the path by combining elements that appear in different places. For example, problem solving, team building, and meetings management will cross different competencies. They only have to be taught once and can then be applied to different competencies.

Turnover

At this point, let's take a little side trip and talk about turnover. What we find in most organizations is that there is a great deal of turnover in the front-line functions. Interestingly, most of it happens in the first sixty to ninety days. Once employees become productive and comfortable in their jobs, they tend to stick around.

Therefore, one of the conclusions you could draw is that if you can bring new employees up-to-speed faster and they become competent and confident earlier, you can head off some of the turnover that happens because new employees become frustrated or bored.

However, there is another type of turnover that you not only want but want to encourage to happen faster. When people are going to be doing a new job for the first time, they often don't understand what they are going to be asked to do each and every day. People who are not happy with their jobs at that level should leave. Another type of turnover we want is internal attrition, where people move to higher value jobs where they can earn more money and take on more challenging roles. Learning Paths help us insulate customers from the impact of this type of attrition as well.

Sometimes employers end up holding people back and paying premium salaries to keep service levels up, only to find frustrated employees and rising operating costs. With a Learning Path strategy you never have to put a new employee in front of a customer until he or she is proficient with that part of the job and has a reliable method to go there quickly.

Because the content is written down, you are less dependent on your senior employees to train the new people so they can continue on their own Learning Paths to higher levels of productivity, at which time you can afford to pay them what they are worth.

One place you see this a lot is in a function like customer service. The expectation is that one is going to be helping people solve problems and that it is a friendly, low pressure environment. You may have heard people say, "I don't want to be in sales. You have to be too pushy. I'd rather be in customer service."

The reality of this job is that you're taking a lot of calls from people with problems. They are often angry and frustrated. In many cases, customer service reps become the front line in enforcing policy and making sure that customers don't "work the system." This happens in other areas as well. People decide they want to go into medicine until they discover that they are going to be around sick people every day.

One of the most interesting examples of this is in the field of commercial collections. At some point early in the job, new employees are faced with the challenge that can be expressed as, "So what you're saying is that you want me to pick up that phone and call someone at home during the dinner hour and ask him for money?" One group of potential collectors will say, "I'm not comfortable doing that." Another group will say, "Give me the phone and let me talk to those deadbeats." The first group quits and the second group stays.

As a result, when you get around to working on that Learning Path, you need to add more of this reality very early in the training, or even at the pre-hire stage, so that those who have a moral objection to making collection calls or making cold telemarketing calls will drop out before you spend a lot of time and money on them.

If you've ever been involved with door-to-door sales, there is a key moment of truth that happens when you say, "Go ring that doorbell and get us in to make a pitch." Once this happens, a large number of potential salespeople won't show up for work the next day. Keep in mind that this isn't as expensive in the first week as it is after you're given that same person three weeks of classroom training. As you set your measurement baselines, it's a good idea to look at turnover. However, keep an eye not only on the turnover rate but also on when it's actually happening.

Summary

Learning Paths are not just for new employees or large organizations. Learning Paths can be structured to move average employees to top performers and to prepare existing employees to move to their next position. The process for mapping out any Learning Path is the same. You need to identify the desired proficiencies and then determine the formal training, practice, and experience needed to attain that level of proficiency.

Using Learning Paths with current employees is an excellent career development tool. A Learning Path can be laid out for moving to a higher level of performance or preparing for the next position. When Learning Paths are in place for all functions, there should be an existing Learning Path already in place.

Finally, Learning Paths can be used for functions even if only one employee is in that position. It's an excellent way to document what's going on in that position and for cross-training someone else in case a second person is needed.

11

Connecting to Business Needs

S O FAR IN THIS BOOK we've presented the methodology of Learning Paths and provided a great deal of how-to information that will help you build Learning Paths for every function and job. Having this foundation in place will enable you to more effectively connect training to business needs. In fact, it can and should be the steppingstone for moving the training function from a support role to a strategic partner for the organization that we call the learning function—to emphasize its broader role.

Business Planning

To explain these statements in a lot more detail, let's look at how business objectives and plans are typically developed and where training usually comes in. At the highest levels in the organization, the long-term course of the business is charted along with macro goals and objectives. These objectives are then the basis for the objectives and plans at the next level. This process flows downhill to the front lines until everyone has a role in making the overall business objectives work. This is the traditional command-and-control model that almost everyone uses.

In addition, these objectives often result from major change initiatives, such as quality improvement, reengineering, business process outsourcing, and acquisition integration. These initiatives have a significant effect on the nature and shape of the workforce that can be greatly simplified by using the Learning Path Methodology.

In the traditional model, various business leaders summon the training manager as they recognize a need to do some training during their planning process. For example, marketing decides that they are going to launch two new products this year. In this plan they determine that they need to train the sales force as well as customer service in how to sell and support these new products. So the training person is called in. Before even talking to training, marketing may have already determined they want a three-day workshop and may have set money in the budget.

This model creates a lot of the variation and duplication that we were trying to drive out as we developed Learning Paths. It is not uncommon in large companies to find completely separate teams developing a course like team building in different business units at the same time, or to see a company buying a different sales skills course for each division or business unit, where a single course could have served all of them. This all happens because the learning function isn't involved early enough in training decisions. In addition, the learning function often is not the recognized owner of how training is done across the company and their knowledge of how learning really happens is underutilized.

In addition to variation and duplication, there are some other drawbacks to the traditional approach. First, it builds in a significant delay and/or creates unrealistic deadlines for the learning function. It's not uncommon for it to take six months to a year to get an approval to build a training program and then to have only thirty days to actually build and test the program. If the decision-making process had been more efficient and had involved learning professionals up-front, the program could have been built, tested, and implemented on a realistic schedule.

Second, the training solution may not really help enable the business objective. It could be that the pre-selected training method is the wrong method. It could also be that the problem or need being addressed really isn't a training issue at all. Perhaps we don't need to have a course on communication skills to improve information sharing. Maybe we just need to put up a bulletin board.

All of this can and should change as we begin to integrate Learning Paths with business needs and when the learning function has a seat at the big table early in the planning process.

For this walkthrough of the business planning process, we are going to assume that we have Learning Paths for all the major functions and jobs. We are also going to assume that, in our work to accelerate those paths, we have already created proficiency models and process maps for each function, and we have done a lot of research into how jobs are actually done. Our last assumption is that we have enough measurement capability to have real-time data on what the people in the workforce know and have the skill to do.

We recommend a careful review of these assumptions on a regular basis and, if any are out-of-date, missing, or inadequate in any way, corrective action should be the first priority.

Role of the Learning Function Leader

As a business leader, if you find yourself in a strategic planning session and your learning leader or chief learning officer is not participating, then you have a problem. Why? Because strategic planning by nature involves change. Something in the organization will change in order to produce a positive outcome. Success invariably depends on changing what people know and what they are able to do. Planning for this has to come ahead of many other decisions, like how many parking spaces or workstations will be needed.

So what does the chief learning officer bring to the table? A proficient learning leader will bring data about knowledge and skills within the organization, analysis about the time and money it takes to change them, and opinions about how to increase profits by accelerating learning and reducing cost.

Planning Process

In order to connect business needs to training, we are going to look at a process that has two key components, a proficiency planning process and a Learning Path planning process. The proficiency planning process takes business and functional leaders through a process that helps them determine what changes will need to be made to the workforce in order to meet their business objectives and plans. The output of that process serves as a starting point for the learning function to look at potential changes to Learning Paths that will result from new business strategies.

What's happening at a high level is the following. First, the business decides to move in a new direction for the next year or more. This is most likely going to require a change in the proficiencies of the workforce. The learning function then determines how these proficiencies can be developed and provides feedback to business leaders on the time and cost of making the change.

This process is greatly simplified and streamlined as a result of all the work that has gone into developing proficiency models and Learning Paths in the first place. That work should provide the organization with current, if not real-time data on what the workforce is capable of doing now.

Proficiency Planning Process

The proficiency planning process takes place with key business and functional leaders. It is led by a senior-level training executive, such as a chief learning officer. There are basically three steps. Figure 11.1 shows them.

Figure 11.1. Proficiency Planning Process

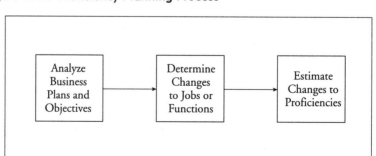

1. Analyze Business Plans and Objectives

In this first step, we meet with business leaders and key stakeholders to understand what changes will be taking place over the next year. We are looking for anything that will

- Change the way jobs are done
- Change performance standards
- Increase the number of new employees
- Change the organizational structure
- Change policies or procedures
- Change, add, or remove products and services
- Change, add, or remove markets and customers

Any of these changes has the potential to drive a change in proficiencies and a change in Learning Paths. For example, if new products will be added, then the current workforce will have to be trained to sell those products and deal with the questions and problems that can result. Take the example of increasing sales goals by 15 percent. This may require that salespeople learn new approaches and sales tactics.

We are trying to avoid making the assumption that the current workforce can and will respond quickly to any business change. For example, say you make the decision that to increase sales you are going to have customer service reps try to sell extended warrantees when customers call with service problems. However, the current pool of customer service reps was hired and trained to be problem solvers and not salespeople. The new sales skills required will have to be either added to a new-hiring profile or will require training. There may also be some attrition because some customer service reps simply don't want to be salespeople.

So the first step is to recognize the change that business plans and objectives will have on what employees must know and be able to do. All of these changes will eventually filter down into training needs.

This is the time to look at any major change initiatives that will lead to major changes in both training and the workforce. These changes might include:

- Installing enterprise-wide software, such as SAP

- Business process outsourcing

- Acquisition and merger integration

- Six-Sigma quality initiative

2. Determine Changes to Jobs or Functions

In this step, you are trying to determine which jobs or functions will be affected by the newly planned actions. Increasing sales by 15 percent may have an effect on both sales and customer service. For example, if sales stimulates more orders, customer service needs to gear up to take those orders.

It's also possible that, as you look at affected jobs and functions, there will be crossovers to other departments or business units. For example, a sales strategy can spill over into production or distribution. It's also likely that there will be some common changes to proficiencies that can be shared as all Learning Paths are revised. For example, there may be some new technical knowledge required or there may be some joint changes to the computer system.

3. Estimate Changes to Proficiencies

The third step is to compare the business change to the existing capabilities of the workforce. In other words, what is the gap between what people know and are able to do today, based on today's business objectives, versus what they will be required to know and be able to do to meet the upcoming business objectives of the future?

This is a process of contrasting the list of changes with the current proficiency model. We can go through this part of the process by asking the following questions:

- Which proficiencies are no longer relevant and can be deleted?

- Which proficiencies will have to be done at a higher level and how much higher?

- What new proficiencies must be added?
- Do any proficiencies have to be recombined, split apart, or rearranged?

For example, let's say that as a result of the new enterprise-wide software, we are going to be able to provide managers with real-time financial information. In the past, they only received this information quarterly, so it wasn't used for the day-to-day operations of the business. Now managers must not only use this software to do queries and generate reports, but they also must be able to use that information to make everyday decisions and tactical corrections to the business plan. However, since it wasn't used this way in the past, we haven't hired anyone with this background. We will need to build all of these skills.

This type of change to the way people do things is often overlooked. Much later, it is uncovered as the root cause of a problem with implementation or one of the reasons that return on investment is not meeting expectations. Later in this chapter we will describe how Learning Paths improve return on investment.

Now we ask different questions up-front, such as what proficiencies will change and how we should change the Learning Path.

Take another example, such as a start-up business or moving a manufacturing facility to another country. You'd need to ask the following questions:

- Does anyone have the background and expertise to move a manufacturing plant?
- Will we be able to hire to a similar job profile or will we need to develop a lot of new proficiencies?

As you look and compare current proficiencies to business plans, ask these additional questions:

- Is this something we can train our people to do? If not, must we hire a different workforce?
- Is there enough capacity in our workforce or will we need to add new employees?
- Will we be able to develop new proficiencies fast enough?

In some cases, the answers to these questions will lead to a change in the business plan. If we can't develop the right workforce fast enough to make a change in the way the plan is stated, the plan must be changed and we must adopt a different approach.

You will find it really helpful in this step if you've done a lot of work to date that helps you understand how work is currently done. You also have a lot of real-time data on what the workforce can do and cannot do. Without real-time proficiency data, decision makers are often out of touch with these realities because they are typically removed from most of the day-to-day operations. They aren't often on the sales floor, in the plant, or visiting customers on a daily basis. Being able to bring this information into a planning session improves the risk analysis process and your ability to avoid potential problems.

Learning Path Planning Process

As we stated earlier, the output of the proficiency planning process is agreement on the changes to proficiencies for those functions and jobs that need to change. By definition, changing proficiencies will cause a related change to a Learning Path. To find these changes to the Learning Path, the learning function meets and works through a three-step process, shown in Figure 11.2.

Figure 11.2. Learning Path Planning Process

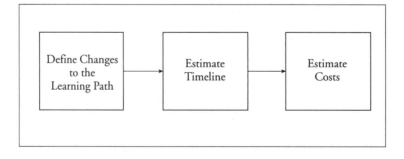

1. Define Changes to the Learning Path

As you look at a change to a proficiency, you have the following options for changing the Learning Path: delete, add, modify, rearrange, regroup, shorten, or extend.

By extending a Learning Path, we mean gearing it toward higher levels of proficiency and/or adding a number of new proficiencies. The job has grown larger so the Learning Path must be extended, for example, when customer service is going to do all of the order taking in the future. In the same respect, when order taking is removed from customer service, the path is shorter.

2. Estimate Timeline

The second step is to determine how long it will take to make the changes to the Learning Path. This is critical because it will relate to the time pressures the business leaders feel. If they need to add five new, major customers in the first quarter, that goal may not be possible if it will take two months to retrain the sales force. Giving this feedback to the business leaders early on may help them decide on a change to the strategy instead of a change to the Learning Path. For example, they may choose to add new salespeople with a different level of experience.

3. Estimate Costs

Many of the changes to a Learning Path will result in new expenditures. When we use the Learning Path approach, we are always looking for the most cost-effective way to do training, rather than just throwing training classes at a problem. Along with the timeline information, we present the cost estimate to senior leadership.

At this point, they know what needs to be done to bring the workforce up-to-speed to meet their objectives, as well as how long it will take and how much it will cost. We stress the point of doing this early in the planning process so that changes to the business strategy can be made if it will take too long or cost too much to prepare the workforce for the business leaders' strategies.

Exhibits 11.1 and 11.2 are examples of the proficiency planning and Learning Path planning processes. You will see how a sales action translates into changes in the Learning Path, and how these changes have the potential to change the business objective.

In this example, the business has decided that one action to increase sales is to begin going after government contracts, something they have not done before. There are no current proficiencies that relate to selling to government agencies, so several need to be added, including being able to respond to government requests for proposals (RFPs) and complying with a code of conduct and ethics specifically for this type of business.

Exhibit 11.1. Proficiency Planning Process

Business Objective #1: Increase sales by $150,000 from government contracts

Proposed Actions	Changes to Jobs or Functions	Change to Proficiencies
1. Respond to government RFPs	Salespeople will be identifying and responding to government RFPs	Complete government RFPs according to the timeline and standards of the government agency Provide cost information in the RFP that meets with company profitability standards
2. Build relationships with procurement agents		
3. Comply with government conduct and ethics rules		

Exhibit 11.2. Learning Path Planning Process

Change to Proficiency	Changes to Learning Path	Timeline	Cost
1. Complete government RFPs according to the timeline and standards of the government agency	• Add self-study on how to respond to RFP	3 weeks	$3,500
	• Add 1-day workshop where an instructor works with salespeople on how to write an RFP	6 weeks	$15,000
	• Find a subject-matter expert who can coach salespeople through their first three RFPs	Unknown (We may need to hire for this)	Unknown
2. Provide cost information in the RFP that meets with company profitability standards			

Let's look at the output of the proficiency planning process through the eyes of senior sales and marketing leaders. The big issue is that there is nobody in the current sales organization who has the experience to coach salespeople on this type of sale. Someone could be developed to do this, but it would take time. Someone may be hired or a consultant may serve in that role.

The exhibit is a very simple example of how we work through one or two small changes to proficiencies for one function. It becomes more elaborate as you work through all of the action items in a business plan for all of the major functions. However, the result of this process is that whatever training is done will be in alignment with current and future business needs. In addition, it allows the business to quickly correct course and change a business strategy, if it's possible within time and budget constraints, to prepare the workforce for the upcoming business change.

Learning Paths and ROI

One of the great debates in training is how to measure business results. It's been expanded to look at not just the results but also the cost of getting those results, in other words, return on investment (ROI). As we've said, it's easy to demonstrate that cutting time out of a Learning Path leads to increased business results because the employee is producing results days, weeks, or even months sooner. There is also an extremely strong multiplier effect as the number of employees on the Learning Path increases. In functions that have 200 or 300 employees even a few days makes a difference.

With that being said, let's look at the results side of the equation. You should be able to train well-qualified employees to do just about anything. However, the results they produce once they are well trained has a lot to do with the strategies the business is trying to implement. Training can prepare individuals to be good at doing a worthless job as well as a meaningful one. A top, well-trained salesperson will produce limited results if he or she is selling the wrong product at the wrong time to the wrong marketplace. They can also do a really good job of selling products that are unprofitable to manufacture and deliver. So, the better sales people do their job, the worse the business results.

It's relatively easy to see the connection between training and performance. You can see and hear the difference in how employees work. How that new performance translates into business results has more to do with the relationship between that performance and the desired outcome. So what you actually need to do first is to demonstrate that the desired performance equals some level of business results. Then, working backward, if performance is increased through training there is a corresponding business result.

On an assembly line it's easier to see how changes produce different outcomes at the end of the line. If employees work faster or reduce errors, there is a measurable increase in production. Therefore, the measurement process needs to work from the business results back to training rather than the other way around. Measure the relationship between performance and business results. If that relationship is satisfactory, build training to achieve that performance and then the change in performance will yield a change in business results.

Now let's look at the cost side. The easiest way to drive the cost out of training is to remove everything that has no effect on performance. That can be everything from eliminating irrelevant information to cutting out lectures that no one will remember to removing self-study that no one completes. It can be as simple as this. Look at a training class where everyone takes a test at the end. The average score is 80 percent on the last day of the training. You give everyone the same test six weeks later and the average score is 20 percent. Maybe the training should only have covered the 20 percent that was retained.

Another way to look at cost is to look at how the training is delivered. A lot of training ends up as an instructor with a stack of PowerPoints. It was easy and quick to develop. However, when you consider the time and expense of putting people in classrooms, it's often the most expensive way of doing training. In particular, because it's so removed from the actual job, you need to do a lot more of it to achieve the same results. This approach is slow to change because it may require an investment today to save money in the long run, which is not an easy argument to make.

What you will find with Learning Paths is that it puts in place the infrastructure to effectively work on business results and ROI. A Learning Path looks at connecting business needs to the desired change in employee performance. It then looks at how to get that performance in the fastest, most effective, and least costly way. The hard and undisputable measure of a Learning Path is the time it takes to get performance to change. Whatever the effect of the change in performance is, you will get more of it sooner with a Learning Path approach.

Organizational Initiatives

Another way to look at connecting Learning Paths to business needs is to consider the major change and organizational initiatives that companies are undertaking on a continuous basis. Setting aside the merits of any of these initiatives, using the Learning Paths Methodology can increase their likelihood of success. In other words, without commenting on whether business process outsourcing is a good or bad idea, Learning Paths make it much easier and effective to move a process from one location to another.

The following is a quick discussion of how to apply the Learning Path Process to various change initiatives. We've included in this list those initiatives with which we have had the most experience.

Centralization

In the past, functions like customer service were often part of another job or done at remote locations. For example, every branch office might have one customer service person or each department had a person who answered customer questions. Top management in many organizations made the decision to centralize the customer service function in a single call center environment. This is made possible and extremely cost-effective due to current computer and communications technology.

However, since these functions were not under a single manager prior to centralization, they were done differently throughout the organization. There may have been some formal customer service training, but it was not around all of the individual processes. Effectively centralizing these functions and training a staff of customer service reps starts with documenting current processes and writing down the knowledge that currently exists.

From that point, Learning Path Teams can define a standardized process for each function based on the input from top performers and any business changes that must be made. This new process then serves as the structure for new training. In other words, the Learning Path is laid out in the way the job is actually going to be done.

As the functions are centralized and new employees enter, there will be a lot of real-time learning going on as the new processes are tried out and the workforce gets up-to-speed. Therefore, it's important to put a maintenance plan in place that will allow for fast updates to the Learning Path.

Mergers and Acquisitions

One of the benefits of mergers and acquisitions is the ability to reduce redundant functions and eliminate duplication. However, this requires blending together two organizations that have different processes, policies, and procedures. Learning Paths help speed this process along in the following ways.

First, a Learning Path would be mapped out for a selected function in each organization. For example, if you had two claims departments, you would map a Learning Path for each. Then the Learning Path Team would go through the process of selecting the best from each path and consolidating them into a new Learning Path.

Second, as you laid out Learning Paths for all of the functions that are being merged, you would start to see a lot of similarity in the training. For example, the same product training will cross many functions. Whatever can be driven into self-study or e-learning can be shared across the organization.

Finally, since this is a time of significant change, it is an opportunity to build a new culture of managers as coaches and mentors. This also may play a role in determining who among the managers will stay and who will not.

Business Process Outsourcing

During business process outsourcing, functions are picked and moved either across town or half-way around the world. Often this can involve the training of just a few people, several hundred, or even a thousand new employees in an extremely short time period. As you can imagine, there is usually a lot of chaos during the transition and when the new locations open up.

Having a Learning Path in place for these functions will make the change easier. Without a Learning Path, what usually goes to the new location is the formal training. Everything about on-the-job training tends to be lost and needs to be relearned, and that takes a lot of time. In addition, all of the training that was never written down or well-documented is lost because the highly trained people often don't make the move or become too busy with other parts of the move.

Finally, we've found that when you move a function or process, all of the flaws go with it. Prior to moving a function or during the move, the processes need to be fixed and then put into a new Learning Path. Business process outsourcing becomes a perfect time to do this type of process reengineering.

IT Enterprise-Wide Solutions

IT enterprise-wide solutions have the potential of providing real-time information on almost every aspect of the business. However, just training new users on how to enter data and run reports is far from sufficient to make them useful.

What's needed is training that mirrors how the technology is going to be used on the job. For example, just because the system allows you to do real-time financial analysis doesn't mean it will happen if it's never been part of the person's job. A new process for how the job will be done in the future is needed, and then training must be built around that new process. In other words, a new Learning Path must be created that blends the technical side of operating the system with the real-time practice and application of how it's going to be used.

Think of all the software capability that sits on most managers' desks. They seldom can operate all of it and often what they do use is only a fraction of the capability. What's missing is the connection to the job with the experience and practice it takes to use it. In other words, the training isn't about using Microsoft Excel to create spreadsheets but rather how to build sales forecasts and present them to upper management.

Lean Manufacturing

We mention lean manufacturing here because the issues are similar to most process improvement initiatives from ISO 9000 to Six Sigma. One of the things that happens in lean manufacturing is that the workplace is totally reorganized for both production and safety reasons. The flow of work is different, employees' jobs are changed, and even the plant floor looks different.

Learning Paths can play an important role by really documenting and measuring the changes in how people work so that they can be used by the next generation of employees. Learning Paths also serve as a valuable tool for blending what was done in the past with what still works in the new workplace.

Summary

Learning Paths enable the learning function to play a more strategic role as business leaders plan out the future. Learning Paths provide management with a tool that gives them real-time information about the capabilities of their workforce and what it will take to make a strategic change. Learning Paths also provides an easy method for measuring and reporting return on investment that will help justify implementing a Learning Paths Initiative.

Finally, Learning Paths can be the missing link that makes many of the improvement initiatives work. The success of these initiatives often depends on blending the actual work with the new processes and structures.

12

Capturing Content

THE ADVANTAGE OF lecture-based training is that you can rely on an expert to provide the content. It doesn't have to be completely written down. However, this is a very inefficient and costly way to deliver information. But as you move away from the expert model to using professional trainers and facilitators you quickly start to lose the depth of information that an expert will have. You also lose the real-time updating that an expert can do.

In a work environment where there are large numbers of employees, you need multiple trainers, which means that there is a lot of variation from one class to the next and from one trainer to another. You could completely script out the training, but we find that most trainers won't stick to a script. In fact, if the script is really good it's questionable whether you need the trainer or not.

You are also going to be faced with significant challenges when experts leave or are promoted. Knowledge that has been passed on informally quickly starts to lose its value. In organizations that are going to be moving functions to new locations or setting up new facilities, this same problem is magnified because of the lack of enough experts to do training.

Another example is what you will commonly see as an organization wants to start building e-learning or Web-based training. In this case, the instructional designer is given all of the current training materials, which are often no more than a large stack of PowerPoint slides. So the designer basically has lots of headlines and unexplained bullet points. In fact, those who have followed the rules of making good overheads have shortened up the bullet points to short sentences and sentence fragments.

All the detailed information that explains what everything means and what's important is missing. That's all still inside someone's head. The result is that the e-learning either looks like an online PowerPoint presentation or the lesson is extremely weak or superficial.

The case for capturing detailed content is very strong. Capturing content systematically and rigorously will help in every part of building Learning Paths and reengineering all of the training events along that path. Let's go into the various techniques that can be used to capture content.

Presentations

One of our past clients was a large, multi-hospital health care organization. Whenever they would have a meeting, at least one person would carry into the room a large stack of PowerPoint overheads, mostly black and white, which then became the focus of the meeting. They would go through thirty or forty overheads in about an hour and then go on to the next meeting. While this may seem extreme, it's probably a standard for a lot of organizations.

The real issue is that a lot of expert content vanishes after each meeting. This content could have been used for training or to build a knowledge management system, but it's never written down. There are two easy ways to capture this information. The first method we use is to audiotape these presentations. We have the tapes transcribed and then cross-referenced to the PowerPoint slides. It's really a matter of writing in where each new slide started. If you want to connect them further, you can even paste the transcripts into the notes pages of PowerPoint.

A second method is to record the presentation directly into each slide. This is really simple. All you need is that small microphone that came with your computer, which you probably stuck in a drawer somewhere. You can also buy a new one for under $10. For this method, we like to use a laptop because we can record everything in the expert's office.

In PowerPoint, under the slideshow drop-down menu, there is a "Record Narration" command. This creates a WAV, or sound file, that appears on the actual slide page. Ask the expert to describe each slide in detail. Do this for every slide so that it has its own sound file. When this is done, you have a rough but completely narrated slide show. And you also have the content you need to build self-study or Web-based training.

Here's a great place to start capturing PowerPoint presentations. In almost every new-hire training, there is a series of department heads or functional experts who provide an overview of what they do. It's always challenging to get enough of these peoples' time, so here's a great opportunity to capture their content.

There is also a lot of variation in what experts present as well as the quality of their presentations. All of the information can be transformed into self-study or other delivery methods once you've captured the actual content. Let's talk about what we do with this content.

Electronic Capture

More and more functions are driven by a computer application. Consider how a computer is used now in order entry, customer service, accounts receivable, reservations, and inventory control. In many of these functions, what happens on the computer coincides with a phone conversation. Use one of two methods to capture this type of content in a way that moves quickly into training, job aides, or online help.

First, select a top performer or someone who can be identified as doing the process correctly. Then ask him or her to list either the most common types of calls he or she takes or the transactions. The person will probably give you some immediate resistance by stating that all calls are different or that there are no "typical" transactions. Everything is an exception. In reality, this is never the case; you just need to push harder until you can agree on some major categories. For example, a customer service center will get a wide range of calls about a lot of different issues. However, the calls tend to group into calls for information, calls with a problem, or something as simple as a customer calling to change an address.

Using the first method, you will ask the top performer to print out the sequence of screens they would use for each call. If a customer calls with a problem, there is a series of screens that are typically used to look up and record information. There may also be some letters or correspondence that is sent out. Working with the top performer, write on each page, step by step, exactly what happens, including the key strokes and the key parts of the conversation.

A second method, which is a little more high-tech, is to use a screen capture video application to make short digital videos that capture what is happening on the screen and what the employee is saying. This software is actually very inexpensive and it will work with any PC-based application. To record the narration, get that microphone out of the drawer again. Ask the top performer to work through an example while describing what's happening. You can even role play a call.

We have found that many people find it difficult to talk and use the computer while you are doing video capture. One way you can address this is to have one person do the computer part while another does the narration. If this isn't possible, tell your star to do the computer part first and then talk through what he or she is doing.

You end up with a library of short videos, usually in an MPEG format, that can be shared either online or on a CD. They can be played in any order, any time you want. You can always go back and polish them up for self-study training. One of the advantages of these videos is that a learner can play them over and over again. They won't get impatient like an instructor will.

Video

There has been a significant change in video recording equipment that makes non-scripted, real-life video not only an acceptable but desirable training and knowledge capture tool. Here is a quick rundown of the differences between digital video and VHS:

- *Stabilization*—Digital video automatically adjusts for the movement of the camera, so you don't get video that bounces up and down. No "Blair Witch" training videos.

- *Lighting*—Digital video can produce bright, sharp images, even in low light. This eliminates the need to carry lights or do a lot of set-up.

- *Clear Audio*—Because the audio track is also digital, it is clear and sharp. With inexpensive remote microphones or lapel microphones, it's not difficult to capture an easily understandable sound track.

- *Desktop Editing*—Digital video can be downloaded directly into your PC, where it can be edited with a low-cost video editing program. This allows you to edit both the video and the audio tracks. It also enables you to compress the file so that it can be placed on a CD or a DVD or sent online.

When using digital video as a capture tool, consider using it for shorter, three- to ten-minute segments. This means that if you are dealing with a larger topic or demonstration, you'll break it into smaller pieces.

This will make it easier for you to work with and edit the video. Hour-long videos are very difficult to watch. So obviously, trying to capture a three-day seminar on video is going to be extremely difficult, if not actually painful, to watch a second time. Here is a short list of some of the better applications for digital video:

- Facility or plant tours

- Demonstrations of equipment

- Sales call simulations

- Interviews with stakeholders

- Visits to customer sites

- Messages from executives

From this list, sales call simulations are particularly effective. As you build your Learning Path for salespeople, you will be identifying both the parts of a sales call as well as the major types of sales calls. Each of these can be role played in short video clips by a top performer. These clips will not only facilitate building new training but can also be used in the training.

Process Mapping

Process mapping is an important tool for understanding how a job or task is done and also for determining how to structure a Learning Path. In addition, as you go through the exercise of mapping out a process, you may identify problems with the process or even see that there really is no standard process at all. Make sure that you fix broken processes before you try to teach them or transport them halfway around the world.

While there are a lot of good process mapping tools, let's go through a simple method that you can use to create a Learning Path. We'll use a customer service call center example, which exists in some form in most organizations. To simplify this example, we will be dealing only with incoming calls.

Step 1: Assemble a Process Mapping Team

Bring together a team of five to ten top performers, first-line supervisors, and selected key stakeholders. These should be people with a lot of hands-on, direct experience with the process.

Step 2: Brainstorm Common Calls

Here is a good way to brainstorm common calls. Give everyone a pack of small self-stick notes. Tell them to write down as many different kinds of calls as they can. Tell them just to complete the sentence, "A customer calls and says. . . ."

As a larger team tries to group the calls into major call types, use larger sticky notes to label each type. In our customer service example, we came up with the display in Figure 12.1.

Figure 12.1. Brainstorming Common Calls

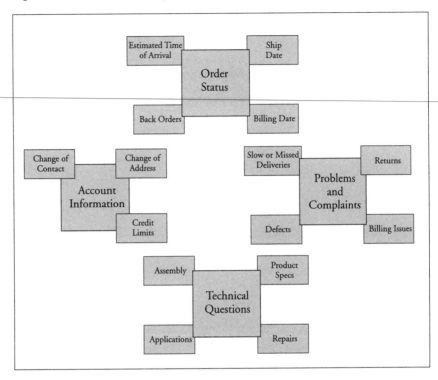

Step 3: Map Out Processes by Call Type

You will find that there is a core process to all calls, and then they vary and branch out after that, based on what the customer wants. It's always easiest to start on the simplest call type. Map it out and then go on to the other call types. This process mapping activity works really well by brainstorming each step in the process and writing the steps down on sticky notes. These can then be arranged and rearranged until there is agreement on how the process is done, as shown in Figure 12.2.

This map shows us a lot about the interaction between the CSR and the customer. We can now identify which screens the CSR needs to be able to access and use. We may want to expand this process to deal with other order status issues, such as what happens when the customer has a problem with a ship date, or what happens if the shipment has been noted as having arrived but the customer can't find it.

Figure 12.2. Process Map

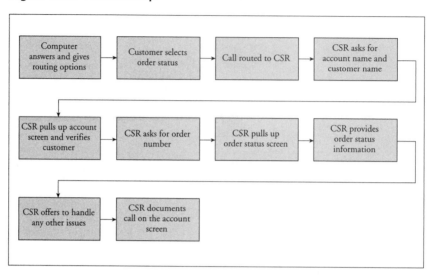

You'll also find, when you start to map out processes, that there is disagreement either about how the processes are done or that they are done in more than one way. Before proceeding, you need to reconcile these differences or else select one way the process is done for training purposes. If these decisions aren't made now they will be made by default by front-line employees. In this example, every time a CSR answers the phone, he or she is making a decision on the best way to do a job. In order to eliminate a lot of variation and even wrong practices, these decisions need to have been made at a higher level.

Step 4: Rank Call Types and Processes

Next, go back and rank all of the call types and processes from easiest to most complex. In our example, order status calls are easier than technical questions. Order status calls are mostly about being able to look up information on a screen. Technical question calls require a lot more knowledge of the products and how they work.

Step 5: Establish an Instructional Strategy

These process maps now become an overall instructional strategy. Sequence the training so that it follows each key process and goes from easiest to complex. For example, the first part of the training is to teach CSRs how to handle order status calls.

CSRs are taught how to handle these calls from start to finish using the phone and computer. They can then begin taking order status calls and become immediately productive; then they go on to learn about other call types. This puts the CSR on the job quickly with early successes. The CSR has become Independently Productive in part of the job in just a few days rather than waiting two or three more weeks before reaching any productivity.

Step 6: Capture Process Information

By laying out this process, you have also identified the information you need to capture. For example, you listed all of the screens that the CSR needs to use. Now you can go out and get a screen capture video of what the CSR actually does with each screen.

In most cases, capturing content is basically a process of documenting what's actually going on. Using the tools and methods we've described will help you a great deal in understanding how the work is done and then short-cutting any revisions or new developments of training. Capturing content also establishes benchmarks and sets a pattern in the organization of writing down information so that it can be easily transferred.

Summary

Capturing content is the cornerstone for improving any Learning Path. It also helps you gain a lot of flexibility in how training can be delivered. In this chapter, we presented a number of ideas for capturing content. Initially this may be a lot of work if nothing has been written down before. However, it's a one-time investment that will pay off in the long term.

While you are capturing content, you can also begin to create training outlines that will fit with each line item on a Learning Path. We will be showing the format for that in Chapter 15, Building Directed Self-Study.

Part III

Doing the "Training Right"

PART III CONSISTS of four chapters that focus on selecting the appropriate training methods for each line item of a Learning Path. While some of this material may seem like basic instructional design techniques, the information is really geared toward improving Learning Paths. For those without a background in instructional design, it will provide new ideas and insights in how training should be built in order to improve the "stick factor" while minimizing cost. The following is a brief overview of each chapter in this part:

Chapter 13: Selecting Training Methods

Chapter 13 provides strategies and templates for determining the most appropriate delivery method for each line item of training. It is focused on three main factors: cost, effectiveness and flexibility.

Chapter 14: Establishing Managers as Coaches

Throughout this book, we've made a big deal out of having managers assume the role of coaches and mentors. As training moves out of the classroom and onto the job, managers play a significant role. This chapter provides ideas and strategies for how to make this transition and how to develop managers as they make the change.

Chapter 15: Building Directed Self-Study

In Chapter 15 we talk about how to move classroom material into self-study. We focus on a template for self-study training, which is critical for building a large volume of consistent training. We also reinforce the concept of directed self-study and the important role managers play.

Chapter 16: Creating the New Classroom Experience

As training is moved out of the classroom and into self-study or field activities, what needs to happen in the classroom changes. In this chapter we describe how classroom training is revised once all of the self-study has been extracted.

13

Selecting Training Methods

AS YOU CAN SEE from our Learning Path Template (Exhibit 13.1), an entire column is set aside to capture how each line item was taught. As you look at a current Learning Path, you're going to see a lot of training done in the classroom. You will undoubtedly also see a lot of other methods being used. Most often, though, the method was selected because it was the easiest to develop, it may be the preferred method of the training function, or it's just historically what has always been done. Seldom do you see anyone go through and take a critical look at how each piece of training should be done.

In general, our preference is to move as much training as possible out of the classroom to where managers and coaches do most of the training. We want to use some form of self-study to provide content that normally would be a lecture or presentation by an expert.

Exhibit 13.1. Learning Path Template

Function: _____   *Date:* _____

Day	What	How	Materials	Done
1				
2				
3				
4				
5				

With that said, it still makes sense to go through every line item and rethink how each piece is delivered. Three factors must be considered. First, which method is most effective? By that we mean selecting the method that will achieve the most learning objectives in the fastest way. We also mean that some training methods are more suited for one particular type of training than another. For example, a classroom setting is much better-suited to building teamwork than giving team members a book to read. The interaction between team members is critical to learning certain skills.

Second, which is the most cost-effective? This is critical when budgets are tight, and training budgets are almost always tight. In other words, does it make sense to fly thirty salespeople to the corporate training center to hold a week-long training class? In this chapter, we'll be presenting a method for looking at training costs and comparing different approaches that will help guide the decision on where to spend the money.

Third, which is the quickest and most flexible? These two factors are lumped together because they really go hand in hand. While there are many old favorites in training that don't change very much, more and more training needs to be developed on a fast track and then maintained and updated continuously. If you are teaching a topic such as how to run a meeting, that content won't change very often and doesn't present much of a time challenge.

However, if you're doing product training in a market that has a six-week product life cycle, like computers, speed and flexibility are critical. We find that there are increasing numbers of training initiatives that involve setting up a customer service center in three weeks or moving a function across the country that require real-time development.

Factor 1: Effectiveness

Let's go back and look at selecting training methods based on what works the best. When CBT (computer-based training) first came out, everyone predicted it would be the cureall for all training. It was supposed to be fun as well as interactive, and there was no topic that couldn't be taught through CBT. You've probably noticed that most companies have virtually no CBT. It turned out that CBT was very expensive to develop. Companies didn't have the infrastructure to support it and, most of all, participants missed the interaction of the live classroom experience.

Now, e-learning is the panacea for training. Everything can be taught over the Web. While this is a vast improvement over CBT, e-learning has it's limitations as well. Maybe a better way to look at it is that, while you may be able to teach everything over the Web, you may not want to. Web training does have the capability for live interaction with other participants and instructors that CBT didn't have, which makes it a better substitute for classroom training. However, it doesn't allow for the direct observation and interaction with a coach, and extensive practice can become extremely tedious over the Web.

In many cases, we will be looking at whether a combination of methods is better than switching methods. If you've ever worked in a manufacturing plant, one of the first things you do is take a factory tour. It's usually loud, busy, and confusing. This is especially true when you have to wear earplugs, a hard hat, and safety glasses. The tour is often given by more than one person. Depending on who gives the tour, you hear, see, and learn different things.

What works better is to create a virtual tour that can be Web-based. You see everything first, either through pictures or short video clips. Then when you go out on the guided plant tour, you know what you're looking at and how everything works together.

As we look at training effectiveness, it's useful to divide training into knowledge acquisition and skill development. Knowledge acquisition spans the gamut from general awareness to recall of facts and figures to being able to use critical information on the job. With knowledge acquisition, we are most concerned about the following:

- Information is current and correct.

- Everyone is getting the same message.

- Information is in a form that is easy to understand.

- Information is limited to what's required for the job to avoid "data dumps."

- Information that is difficult to remember can be easily referenced, as needed.

- Questions are answered in a timely manner.

- Complex concepts can be discussed and clarified.

- Retention and application of information can be tested.

As you look at this list, you begin to recognize that only a few of the items require live interaction with other participants or an instructor. In fact, some of it doesn't require formal training at all. If all I want you to do is remember which key strokes to use to enter a customer order, I probably can just give you a temporary cheat sheet.

e-Learning, print self-study courses, audio, and video are excellent methods for knowledge acquisition. All of these methods ensure that the message is consistent each and every time it is given, which is usually not the case in a classroom.

Depending on the production values and how each method is produced, e-learning, printed self-study courses, audio, and video can all be easily updated. Print is probably the easiest to update, while high-production-value audio and video are the most difficult. As we discussed earlier, short, real-life digital videos are fast and easy to produce, toss out, or update. Full production videos with actors and sets should only be used for training with a multi-year shelf life.

e-Learning has some unique advantages because you can add chat rooms and bulletin boards for discussing content. Also, testing can be much more interesting and engaging, as well as making it easier to gather and maintain test results.

Perhaps the biggest issue we see when companies want to move to something like e-learning is that the content needed has never been captured and written down. A stack of PowerPoint slides is a long way from an e-learning lesson. We often recommend, as an interim step in moving from classroom to another media, that you first build self-study reading assignments. This ensures that all the content you will need is written down.

On the other hand, skill development is a much different task. You can learn all about how to make an effective presentation in some form of self-study. However, knowing how to make a presentation and actually making a presentation are two different things. Knowing how to hit a golf ball three hundred yards and actually being able to hit it that far are two very different things. What's missing are the hours of practice and feedback. You actually have to give a number of presentations and get feedback from a coach. This is something that needs to be done both in the classroom and on the job.

Another increasingly popular way to work on skill development is through a simulation, which is often cheaper and allows for a lot of practice in a safe environment. Some excellent technology is available today that helps you build simulations for call centers. You can practice the conversation and learn the computer system at the same time. With the use of voice recognition software, these simulations are very real.

As we go through each line item on our Learning Path, we want to see whether we can move anything that is knowledge acquisition to some type of reference guide or self-study. Then we want to look at anything that involves skill development and determine whether it should be done in a classroom, on the job, or in simulation. Keep in mind that effectiveness is only one part of the equation. Let's go on to look at the other two factors.

Factor 2: Cost

As we analyze the cost of training, we want to look at it in three ways. First, what's the cost of development? Second, what's the cost of delivery? Third, what's the cost of maintenance and updating?

The actual cost of designing training is very similar across methods unless you choose a freewheeling presentation format. That means sending the expert into the room with the stack of PowerPoint slides. However, to put together training that will actually work requires design work, which includes writing out learning objectives, creating activities, and determining how to deliver content.

The big variation in the cost of training development is in production. As we've stated before, real-life digital videos are cheap to produce, while full-production-value video is expensive. Fully animated, highly interactive e-learning is expensive. Creating e-learning using an existing template can be inexpensive. In general print-based self-study, reference materials, and classroom materials will be on the low end of development costs, while full online simulations will be on the high end.

In addition, you always have the option not to develop training at all but to buy an off-the-shelf product. This is often a good option in teaching soft skills, which are for the most part generic content. Also, let's take a topic like providing an industry overview. Many of the industry trade organizations have already built overview training. For example, in the paper and packaging industry, the leading trade organization has done a nice job of building orientation videos and CD-based lessons.

Often, the bulk of the training dollars are spent in training delivery. Self-study programs, including e-learning, have a big cost advantage on the delivery side. In typical classroom training you have the additional costs of travel, trainer expense, lost time from work, and facilities expenses. As the number of employees to train and the distance from the training location increase, the cost of classroom training quickly outstrips the development cost of other forms of training.

Earlier we talked about using short training meetings with a coach. These are low on delivery cost because they are often added to other regular meetings. They have the additional benefit of being local and just-in-time, meaning they happen where the students are and when they need it.

Another advantage is that we often post self-study reading assignments on a website as downloadable Word documents. As a result the cost of delivery per student, if they decide to print the assignments out, is just a few dollars. You can compare your own training costs by using the template we provide in Exhibit 13.2. Again, you will need to look at both development and delivery costs to determine which is the most cost-effective. We have found that most organizations can save money and time by focusing on content that is truly unique, either to their organization or to the specific job. Use generic training for the rest and invest first in capturing the unique content in words.

Factor 3: Speed and Flexibility

The final factor to consider relates to development time and how easy it is to deploy and update. Let's talk about the speed factor first. The only way to keep training current and relevant is to be able to develop it quickly. However, there are a lot of speed barriers that really have little to do with actual development.

Take a look at the timeline for developing a one-day seminar. It can take several months to a year just to get executive sponsorship and budget approval. At the other end, if there are a number of reviews and approvals required, this can take a few weeks to never. Most instructional designers are familiar with the black hole of the legal department, which can sit on approvals for months on end. These time issues are constant for all training, and we addressed them in detail in Chapter 11, Connecting to Business Needs.

With this said, some types of training will take longer to develop than others. In general, we think of anything that is print-based as being faster to develop than other methods. However, we've discussed that using some of the new technology will make other methods just as fast. We can do some nice digital videos in a few hours.

Exhibit 13.2. Cost Elements

	Classroom	On the Job	One-on-One Tutorial	Practice	Coaching	Simulations	Synchronous Self-Study e-Learning	Asynchronous Self-Study Text Online
Staff Salaries								
Planners/Leaders								
Developers								
Instructors								
Subject-Matter Experts								
Students								
Programs								
Tuition/Fees								
Materials								
Maintenance/Updates								
Contract Developers								
Contract Instructors								
Travel								
Planners								
Developers								
Instructors								
Subject-Matter Experts								
Students								
Facilities								
Offices								
Classrooms								
On the Job								
Equipment								
Systems LMS								
Learning Mgmt System								
Office Supplies								

What's really more critical for speed than the actual method used is to put in place an infrastructure with enough templates so that content, as it's generated, can be dropped into place. Even something as simple as pre-making decisions about type styles and page layouts saves a lot of time.

Another way to increase speed is to build training in smaller, one- and two-hour parts or modules. These modules can then be reused in other training or discarded when out-of-date without destroying the overall integrity of a training program.

Let's say that a new computer program is coming online in three weeks. This program is basically used for ten different customer transactions, including change of address and account status. You create ten screen capture videos that walk through each operation. You create a menu of operations with links to each video in PowerPoint. You place the presentation on a CD. This might take as long as two days. Now if anything changes you can just drop out a screen capture video and replace it.

The flexibility issue is another story. Training is most useful if it can be delivered to any size audience at any time. This becomes a problem when there are a lot of remote locations or when it takes weeks or months to get enough new employees to start a class. Moving to formats that have a lot of self-study or on-the-job training helps solve this problem.

We've also found that there is a problem when any type of technology is involved. It seems that the farther a student is from the home office, the older the equipment and the slower the connection. If you want to play a video in the home office, you'll find VCRs everywhere. But in the Tulsa branch, they'd have to rent one. In other companies, in order to save money they've stripped out the video and audio cards when purchasing computers, which makes it nearly impossible to do online training.

Exhibit 13.3 is a summary planning sheet that will help you determine which training method to use as you go through each line item of a Learning Path.

Exhibit 13.3. Comparison of Training Methods

Method	Effectiveness	Cost	Speed	Flexibility	Barriers
Job Aid					
Training Meetings					
Self-Study Reading					
e-Learning					
Video					
Audio					
Classroom					
Other					

Summary

In this chapter, we presented a process for evaluating every line item in a Learning Path to make sure that the training method selected was appropriate from both an effectiveness and a cost standpoint. Interestingly, what makes it possible to easily move from one method to another will be whether or not the content has been written down. Going from classroom to e-learning is a significant challenge when all the content is in the heads of several instructors.

In the next chapter, we are going to look at how changing the manager's role to that of a coach or mentor makes training more effective. As we've stated before, in order to make self-study or on-the-job training work it requires that managers be actively involved. So as you look at changing training methods, you also need to look at how it will change the manager's role.

14

Establishing Managers as Coaches

AS YOU BEGIN to reduce classroom time, the training function starts to shift away from trainers to supervisors and managers. For example, all of the self-study needs management follow-up to make sure that it has been completed and that it is understood. We've placed the manager's role in relation to Learning Paths under the label of coaching.

Motivator

We like to assume that every new employee comes to work wanting to do a good job and to succeed. However, there are always obstacles and barriers that affect each employee's motivation to learn. A good coach will be aware of these motivation changes and step in to get the employee back on track.

We used to teach new salespeople how to set up appointments with potential prospects. This is a relatively simple skill that can be taught in a few hours. What would happen is that the new salespeople would follow the script and, after a few phone calls, they started to make appointments.

This would go on for a few days until they began to talk about their work with families and friends, who would then convince them that they couldn't just call up the president of a small company and make an appointment because they were brand new and inexperienced.

As a result, the salespeople's confidence would plummet and, suddenly, they would stop getting appointments. This situation required a coach to recognize what was happening and step in, not as a manager but as a motivator, to help restore confidence.

When you work in a call center, you see this phenomenon all the time. After a few weeks of classroom training, new employees are ready to get to work. They may even have mastered taking calls in the classroom. However, when they start to interact with customers, everything changes. Real customers can act in odd and unplanned ways. This is because we never have a chance to put customers through training, so they don't know how to follow the customer script.

The result is a sudden and significant drop in confidence, sometimes to the point where the new employee feels that he or she will never be able to do the job. This is, in fact, where most of the early turnover comes from. This is where the coach needs to step in and be a motivator.

In many companies, you will see the "sink or swim" method of training new employees. There are a lot of sales-related positions where the only form of training is to give the new salesperson a phone book and a phone and tell him or her to start making calls. A few salespeople get some early successes and survive, while there is a 70 to 90 percent turnover of the sinkers. Without changing the training but by adding coaches, the number of swimmers rapidly increases. The coaches are able to get the new employees through the natural and predictable loss of confidence that comes with learning anything new.

Of course, part of being a motivator is to be a cheerleader. Cheerleaders express their hopes that others will do well. They also provide a lot of praise and adulation when there is a success. Where many managers make a mistake is that they only praise perfection or success. That practice misses the point that you need to build confidence in order to reach perfection. We need to shape behavior by reinforcing even small movements in the right direction. This is a skill that coaches can learn and practice.

The way we learn is through a series of "successive approximations." In other words, every time you try something you learn a little more and make fewer mistakes. This goes back to why practice is so important. Let's assume you're doing some type of assembly work.

Over the first fifty assemblies, you'll see a gradual improvement of the finished product. You also might see that, on assembly 25, the employee gets frustrated and gives up. Obviously, in this process you don't want to wait until the end to offer praise and rewards. You need to offer words of encouragement early and often.

Teacher

Coaches are the teachers in the on-the-job classroom. All too often, coaches limit their roles to telling others what they did right and what they did wrong while occasionally throwing in some applause.

Coaches need to be much more active and structured in teaching new employees how to do their jobs. We spelled out all of the on-the-job training that needs to be done in the Learning Path, but it all should be guided by a coach. Let's go through each of the activities that coaches, as teachers, need to master.

Demonstration

An important part of learning is to be able to see and hear how something is done correctly. This could include making sales calls jointly, observing someone else complete a transaction, watching how to fix something, or observing a role play. If the coach is not the expert, then the coach needs to arrange a demonstration by someone who is.

Learning Experiences and Drills

When a coach recognizes that demonstration alone won't be sufficient, the coach must create or apply different learning experiences or drills that will provide a learning experience. This includes adapting some of the old classroom activities into one-on-one training. This might include:

• Role plays

• Creating a game or a competition

• Pairing up with a more experienced employee

• Doing a joint presentation

• Undertaking a research project

• Visiting other locations, departments, or customers

Job Aids

Job aids help new employees remember key facts, concepts, or processes. We like to use what we call "reminder cards." These are simply 3-inch by 5-inch cards with a small amount of information on each one. Reminder cards are posted where employees can see them while they work. They are kept until employees no longer need them and then are thrown away.

Other types of job aids might include:

• Fact sheets

• Price lists

• Lists of questions to ask

• Online help

• Short digital videos

• Reference guides

• User manuals

• Self-study reading assignments

Debriefing

A coach adds value to every piece of training or learning experience by taking the time to debrief it with the employee. To be able to debrief training, it's critical that the coach know what's in that training, and it's even better if the coach has personally attended the training. Debriefing is not the same as testing. It's an opportunity for the employee to process what he or she has learned and clarify any misunderstandings. When building training or learning experiences, it's useful to write debriefing questions to guide coaches. In some cases, we actually build a coaches' guide to go with classroom, online, and self-study training. Some of the key debriefing questions that we use include:

- What insights or new ideas did you get from this training?

- What do you think will be the most useful on the job?

- What did you find to be the most difficult or challenging?

- Was there anything that didn't seem relevant or useful?

- Can you summarize for me what you learned?

- Was there anything you disagreed with or didn't understand?

Training Meetings

As we said earlier, weeks of classroom training can be very ineffective. One method that can easily replace formal classroom training is short training meetings.

Several years back, we launched a training program for new salespeople called the 45-Minute Sales Meeting Series. In essence, we divided basic sales training into weekly sales meetings. Each meeting focused on one topic or skill. In every meeting, there was a brief presentation with one practice activity. At the end, participants were given a practice activity for the week. At the start of the next meeting, there was a debriefing of the week's successes and challenges.

These short meetings were very effective because they were highly focused and included a lot of practical application and practice. The series was flexible enough so that we could hold two or even three meetings a week, if we wanted to. Also, a coach or manager could lead them without a lot of classroom training experience.

This approach can be applied to most work environments. For example, in a call center you could hold a meeting on each call type. In a manufacturing plant, you could hold weekly safety meetings, covering protective equipment one week and safe lifting another.

Exhibit 14.1 is an outline of an agenda that we use to build training meetings. Notice how short and simple the items are.

These meetings don't need to take a lot of time. You can design them to be anywhere from fifteen minutes to an hour in length. They can be included with regular staff meetings or as part of a training lunch.

Exhibit 14.1. Training Meeting Agenda

Topic: (Name of Topic)

Learning Objectives: (One or two things you expect to accomplish)

I. Introduction

    a. Purpose of the meeting

    b. Agenda

    c. Review of any previous meeting

II. Presentation

    a. New content

    b. Questions and discussion

III. Practice Activity

    a. Apply the content in the meeting

    b. Assign follow-up field activity

Evaluation and Feedback

For learning purposes, evaluation and feedback are not the same as a performance evaluation. Feedback is critical for guiding the learning process and is most useful when it's not tied to performance or salary reviews. Coaches need to be able to set up a rapport with the new employee that allows them to tell the new employee what he or she is doing right and doing wrong without fear of bad consequences.

As we've discussed, people don't start by doing things perfectly. Instead, they progress through trial and error as well as repetition. This process speeds up when the coach prevents the employee from repeating the same mistake or gives feedback on what isn't working.

When people are left alone to learn something they often start to make adjustments or take shortcuts. This leads to errors they are unaware of and variations in processes. A coach can keep employees on track so that they learn the process right, and then later, if the employee has discovered improvements, these can be incorporated into the training and learned by everyone.

We were working in a call center several years back and we heard the following conversation:

"Finally, I'd like to offer you our how-to booklet at a special promotional price of just $10.95. It's not really worth it. Would you like one?"

We decided to investigate. We said to the employee that this seemed like a strange way to offer a special promotion. The employee stated that she didn't really know how to place that order in the system but in order to get a perfect call evaluation, she had to offer it. Her approach solved both problems.

This might be an extreme adjustment but, without a coach's continuous evaluation and feedback, these things happen all the time. If you want to see this for yourself, go to a golf driving range some time. You'll see a lot of funny swings, odd stances, and weird grips. Most of these people are self-taught and, through a series of adjustments, they come up with a way to hit the ball. However, these adjustments prevent them from becoming good players.

Another part of evaluation and feedback that can be extremely powerful is to use self-evaluations as learning activities. A self-evaluation helps an individual build awareness of what he or she is really doing.

For example, one of the issues we wanted to address with travel agents was to get them to offer to book a car or hotel for a customer and not just airfare. When we asked them if they offered car and hotel, they usually said that they offer it all the time. However, when we monitored their calls, we found it was less than half the time. This discrepancy can lead to a significant dollar loss for the travel agency.

The issue was that the agents' lack an awareness of what they are doing. We came up with a ten-call self-evaluation that looks like Exhibit 14.2.

What tended to happen was that in the first few calls, there was a mix of yeses and nos. About half-way through the employee started to recognize that he or she wasn't doing as well as he or she had thought and started to make a correction. Soon, all were yeses. Once the employee felt that he or she had made the correction, he or she simply threw the self-evaluation out.

An interesting self-evaluation that we use with salespeople is focused on spending more time listening than talking on a sales call. The self-evaluation looks like the one in Exhibit 14.3.

On the first several calls, salespeople are surprised to find out that they do 75 percent of the talking. As we know, it's very hard to listen when you're talking all the time.

Exhibit 14.2. Self-Evaluation Sample 1

Calls	Self Evaluation #1: I offered car and hotel on this call									
	1	2	3	4	5	6	7	8	9	10
	Yes No	Yes No	Yes No	Yes No	Yes No	Yes No	Yes No	Yes No	Yes No	Yes No

Exhibit 14.3   Self-Evaluation Sample 2

Self Evaluation #1: Who did more of the talking on this call?									
1	2	3	4	5	6	7	8	9	10
You or the Customer	You or the Customer	You or the Customer	You or the Customer	You or the Customer	You or the Customer	You or the Customer	You or the Customer	You or the Customer	You or the Customer

Coaching the Coaches

In larger departments, several managers or supervisors will be doing the same job. For example, there may be twenty sales managers, fifteen store managers, fifty customer service supervisors, or ten production supervisors. In order to make sure that processes are done consistently from employee to employee and work group to work group, it's critical to standardize the coaching.

For example, in most organizations each sales manager will evaluate a sales call differently. In fact, what might be right for one manager is wrong for another. Here are some ideas that we've used to make coaching a consistent and integral part of how training is done:

Coach-the-Coach Sessions

Set aside about an hour a week for coaches to meet in a coach-the-coach session. The first part of this session is an informal discussion of successes and new insights, plus any new coaching challenges. This is a good time to discuss new learning experiences that have worked well or new techniques for addressing any common coaching challenges.

The second part of the session should be set aside for observing and evaluating performance as a team of coaches. For example, if you brought in tapes of phones calls and rated them, after a while the ratings between coaches should start to be more alike. The team can also come up with common standards for observing and rating performance.

Tools, Templates, and Methodologies

Find a common method or way of training employees. Use templates and other tools that everyone uses and updates. For example, training meeting outlines, reminder cards, and self-evaluations are all training tools that go along with a common methodology of teaching through smaller, continuous training events. You are limiting the amount of instructional design experience required by making all the key design decisions in advance.

Keepers of the Process

It's critical to teach the same processes in the same way throughout the organization. As new ideas emerge or there are other changes, such as policy changes, processes will start to vary. It's important to have one person assigned to be the keeper of the process. In other words, this person accumulates all the changes and updates all the coaches on how the process can and should change. If there are undesirable changes or just change for change's sake, the keeper of the process needs to step in and restore the process.

Keep in mind that change itself doesn't necessarily make anything better. Sometimes a change results in accomplishing the same task in a slightly different way but with exactly the same result. The keeper of the process must guide the coaches through selecting one process that everyone will use, rather than having several similar processes. It's easy to improve one process. It's difficult to improve many.

Super Coach

We sometimes call this person the "coach's coach." In other words, one person is assigned to develop and train managers as coaches. This person is also responsible for the overall coaching methodology, as well as keeping everyone on the same page. The Super Coach actually needs to model the coaching process by applying it to the development of managers and supervisors into coaches. This means having a Learning Path and guiding coaches down that path.

Coaching, like most other skills, takes experience and practice to develop. However, this is perhaps the most important skill for a manager or supervisor to have in order to successfully implement Learning Paths. It is the best way to connect what happens in the classroom with the job as well as being able to add the depth of experience that only managers and supervisors have.

Coaching Guide

To help implement the high level of coaching necessary, we create a coaching guide for every Learning Path. This is a basic instruction booklet on how to take a new employee through a specific Learning Path. It takes some time to build the first coaching guide because you will need to include a lot of background information that hasn't been written down yet. However, each subsequent coaching guide is only a customization of the first. Adding the specifics of a new Learning Path are a simple cut-and-paste operation. Use the template in Exhibit 14.4 to develop your own coaching guides.

We can't overstress the importance of coaching and using managers as coaches. This is the best way to tie what needs to be learned to the job. It shortens the Learning Path because you don't need to wait for a scheduled

---

Exhibit 14.4. Coaching Guide

I.   Introduction to Learning Paths

    a.   What is a Learning Path?

    b.   Why are we using Learning Paths?

    c.   Your role as a coach

II. (Function Name) Learning Paths

    a.   Copy of the Learning Path

    b.   Copy of course outlines that correspond to each path

    c.   How we are measuring this Learning Path

III. Coaching Guidelines

    a.   Coaching directed self-study

    b.   Debriefing after classroom sessions

    c.   Conducting on-the-job training

    d.   Building job aids

IV. Tracking and Reporting Progress

    a.   Evaluations and testing

    b.   Keeping new employees on track

    c.   Reporting results

classroom event. While waiting for a class to start, this eliminates problems from a lack of training.

While managers are often reluctant to spend a lot of time coaching, making sure that employees know what to do and how to do it is the fundamental role of a manager. If this isn't happening, you may need to review the manager's job and goals to find ways to free up some time for coaching. Often, managers are burdened with a lot of administrative tasks and paperwork that may be unnecessary or can be delegated to someone else.

In many organizations, managers are hired or promoted not because of their expertise but rather because of their managerial skills. For example, many organizations won't promote their best salesperson into the position of sales manager. However, one of the best ways to learn anything is to teach it. If the sales manager is put into the role of coach, he or she will quickly develop a lot of the expertise that was missing. It will also make the person a better manager because he or she will understand the job being supervised even better. In the short term, the manager may need to work with a subject-matter expert to get up-to-speed. When we look at Learning Paths for managers, coaching experience is a critical part of their development.

Summary

In order for any training to be effective and really stick, managers must be actively involved and support it on the job. The key role managers must play is to be active coaches for on-the-job training, including guiding employees through a Learning Path.

In many organizations, this role for managers will be a significant change and it will only happen if there is clear top management direction and support. This may even include changing management job descriptions and compensation.

On the other hand, managers don't need to be professional classroom trainers or instructional designers. Instead, those professionals should be providing support, materials, and training for managers so that they can become first-rate coaches. The next chapter is on Building Directed Self-Study. Everything we recommend in that chapter is really based on the willingness and ability of managers to support it.

15

Building Directed Self-Study

SELF-STUDY READING assignments are a critical part of accelerating a Learning Path. They also help standardize what new employees are being taught. Self-study assignments begin the process of reducing classroom time and quickly help to reduce overall training costs.

When we talk about self-study, we mean *directed* self-study. This means that there is a time and place set aside for completing the self-study. Management also provides clear direction and support on how and when the self-study will be completed.

In this chapter, we will go step by step through the process of building and implementing self-study reading assignments. All of the techniques that we've used for capturing content will be very useful to you as you create your own.

Definition

We define a self-study reading assignment as a single topic document that, with tests and activities, can be completed in about two hours. The goal is acquisition of knowledge. These assignments are not designed to build skills, but are used in combination with other training to develop skills. For example, we can read about how to close a sale, but developing the skill will take additional practice and coaching. It may even require some classroom time.

Self-study reading assignments also have the advantage of allowing participants to go through training at any time and in any location. In addition, these assignments are easy to update and maintain.

In a typical new-hire situation, we usually end up with between twenty and forty such assignments. That's forty to eighty hours of training. We standardize the format and instructional design to make them easy to develop, but also to allow the student to go through them quickly once they become familiar with the format and learn how to take the tests and report their results.

Development Process

All self-study reading assignments are written as Word documents so that they can be easily uploaded and downloaded from a website and then either printed out or read off a computer screen. Such assignments are an excellent interim step to building e-learning because you've captured the content and have already done some of the preliminary instructional design. Let's look at the steps.

Step 1: Identify Topics

The first step is to go through each line item on your Learning Path and identify any topic currently taught in a classroom that is mostly knowledge acquisition. Topics might include industry overview, company history, product profiles, technical background, or finance. Often, these are the presentations made by the experts. We'll call these people subject-matter experts (SMEs).

Step 2: Outline

We create a one-page outline like the one shown in Exhibit 15.1.

Exhibit 15.2 is an example of an outline for a customer service self-study reading assignment.

Once you write an outline, have it reviewed by an SME to make sure that it is current, correct, and complete. It's better to make these changes now than after you've spent a lot of time writing.

Exhibit 15.1. Outline Format

Title: (Same as the topic)

Overview: One paragraph summary that includes the purpose

Objectives: Two to five learning objectives that are strictly knowledge acquisition

Current Outline: Usually, three to four major subtopics with supporting point... For example:

I. Subtopic 1

    a. Supporting point

    b. Supporting point

    c. Supporting point

II. Subtopic 2

    a. Supporting point

    b. Supporting point

    c. Supporting point

III. Subtopic 3

    a. Supporting point

    b. Supporting point

    c. Supporting point

Exhibit 15.2. Sample Outline

Topic: Call Center Overview

Overview:

The purpose of this assignment is to provide a big-picture look at the customer service call center. It describes what happens in the call center and how the call center is set up in order to best serve our customers.

Objectives:

As a result of this assignment, new CSRs will be able to:

- Explain the purpose and objectives of our call center
- Describe the physical setup of the call center
- List and explain the types of calls customer service gets and how they are routed to CSRs

Content Outline:

I. Introduction

    a. Purpose and goals

    b. Past, present, and future

    c. Your role as a CSR

II. Call Center Layout

    a. Customer service computer system

    b. Workgroups and teams

    c. Work rules

III. Types of Calls

    a. Incoming calls

    b. Call routing

    c. Call handling process

In an ideal situation, you would not only write an outline for each self-study reading assignment but also for every line item on the Learning Path. This would help you identify duplication as well as make sure that you have covered everything. If you decide to write these additional outlines, make sure to add the following information:

- *Time:* How long it takes
- *Method:* How the training is delivered
- *Target Audience:* Who the training is for

While this may seem like a lot of work initially, most of your work is a one-time investment that will pay off substantially in the long term. In the future, you will be adding a few outlines and updating the ones you already have. You won't be writing them all at the same time again.

Instructional Design Template

As we've said, it's important to have an instructional design template to develop self-study assignments in quantity, and also to make it easier on the students, who will quickly become familiar with how to use them. Basically, there are four key elements of our design:

- Set-Up Activity
- Text
- Application Activity
- Tests

Set-Up Activity

The purpose of the set-up activity is to get the student ready to learn about the topic being presented. One approach is to ask for the student's ideas and opinions about that topic. We know from adult learning studies that adults have opinions about everything. These opinions can often be barriers to learning something new that will require the learner to change his or her opinion. So getting these opinions out early and dealing with them up-front speeds up the learning process. Some of the ways you can do this include:

- Ask three to five open-ended discussion questions, including what they like best and least about the topic. Always leave space in the document for participants to write in their answers.

- Tell the students to describe their experiences with the topic, such as the last time they called a customer service center with a problem. What happened? What did they like best? What did they like least?

- Tell the students to look at something, for example, a website, part of the plant, or people working in a call center. Tell the students to write down their impressions of what they saw.

- Tell the students to interview someone else, such as an expert. Give them a list of interview questions to ask.

Another approach is to create a knowledge pre-test. This should be done in an entertaining way, for example, using a puzzle or a game. Crosswords and circle-the-word games work really well for this type of activity.

The set-up activity should be short and focused. It should take twenty minutes or less to complete. Remember, the entire assignment should take about two hours. If it has to be longer, consider making it into two assignments.

Text

The core of any self-study reading assignment is the text. It's important that the text be written in a friendly, easy-to-read manner. Guidelines for the text portion include:

- Write in the second person. Write as if you are talking directly to the student sitting at a table beside you. Always use a conversational style, which is easier to read and to write.
- Use lots of bullets, large text, and plenty of white space. This will make the text visually easier to read, especially for older audiences, who will really appreciate the larger text.
- Avoid cluttering up the text with lots of boldface, underlining, quotations, and italic. What tends to happen is that everything seems to be highlighted and thus the emphasis you want to give it is lost.
- Use lots of subheads. Try to avoid page after page of text that isn't divided by subheads. The subheads should follow the logical flow of the text.
- Avoid policies and procedures. This is not a policy and procedure manual. Don't cut and paste those materials into the text. Either rewrite what you want to say or direct the student to go read the policy and procedure manual. This also helps with content management because you won't have to change the training every time the procedures are modified or expanded.

Self-study reading assignments also provide you with an opportunity to interact with the readers and ask them to do something related to the text. Here are some examples:

- Ask readers to add to the list. Often, you will have included a list of ideas or examples; ask the readers to write in ideas and examples of their own.
- Link to something else. Ask them to read another document, visit a website, or even watch a video. Always give them three or four questions to answer about what they found in those links.

Application Activity

Students should always be directed to do something with the new knowledge they have gained. Application activities can also be prework for an upcoming classroom session. Examples of application activities include:

- Write an action plan.

- Answer questions about a short case study.

- Make a presentation.

- Make or take calls.

- Evaluate your next ten calls.

- Watch someone else do the task and write up your observations.

Tests

We use two types of tests in self-study reading assignments. First, we use short, five-question knowledge checks. These are self-scored, either multiple choice or true/false, placed at the end of each section of the text. If the student has read the section, he or she will be able to score 100 percent on these knowledge checks. If not, he or she should go back and reread the section.

Second, we use a final test. This is a fifteen-to-twenty-item test that is usually multiple-choice. Again, we are testing knowledge acquisition. In some cases, where a learning management system is up and running, these tests can be placed online. This increases compliance and lets you know how each student is doing.

Compliance and Motivation

Compliance and motivation is a significant issue that you will face when moving from classroom to self-study. While classroom learning has significant issues with retention, self-study has significant issues with compliance. In other words, people won't go through the self-study or spend the time with it that they should. Therefore, we always implement "directed self-study," either blending self-study with coaching or on-the-job training, or presenting it as prework for the classroom. This means that a manager or supervisor will be involved with the students as they go through the material.

We have found that compliance goes up and the employees actually complete the assignments when their managers make it part of the job and follow up on progress. This means setting aside time and space for self-study and, in some cases, letting the employees leave the workplace or go home to complete assignments. The coach's guide should include follow-up questions to be used in debriefing sessions.

Summary

Moving content out of the classroom and into self-study helps to preserve classroom time for more productive activities than lectures and presentations. Self-study also provides the flexibility of delivery anywhere at any time.

One of the major challenges in building self-study is that most of the content has not been written down. However, once it's been captured it provides an ongoing database of knowledge that can be easily updated. In many respects this is a first step to creating any e-learning.

However, with self-study alone the problem is getting employees to actually read and understand it. That's why directed self-study is critical. Management must play an active role in monitoring and debriefing self-study. Managers must be provided with training and materials to perform this role.

In the next chapter, Creating the New Classroom Experience, we show how managers can take a more active role in the training, which places less emphasis on platform training skills and more on practical hands-on experience.

16

Creating the New Classroom Experience

IN PREVIOUS CHAPTERS, we've stressed the importance of selecting the right training methods by effectiveness, cost, speed, and flexibility. We have also changed the focal point. We looked beyond what would get us to graduation faster, cheaper, better. Now we are focusing on proficiency, when the students are actually able to do the job. This changes everything, including the way we use classroom training.

By applying these principles, we've been able to move a lot of training out of the classroom and into other delivery methods. In particular, we've moved most of the knowledge acquisition from the classroom into some form of self-study.

This leaves us with a major dilemma. What do we do with all the classroom training that's left over? In other words, without all of the lectures and presentations, all we have left are activities and exercises. There may be a lot of valuable training left, but it no longer hangs together as a seminar or workshop.

In this chapter, we are going to look at a range of ideas, templates, and strategies that can help you quickly transform what you have into a new classroom experience that will be highly effective and will take less time. We'll also look at some of the challenges you will face in getting students to accept and participate in this different type of classroom experience.

Let's start with a big-picture look at how the training experience changes by looking again at a sales training example. A typical sales training program is covered in a three-to-five-day workshop. (*Note:* The terms *seminar* and *workshop* are often used interchangeably. We'll use the word seminar when we are talking about a training session that is mostly lecture and presentation. We'll use workshop to refer to something that is more interactive and includes a range of activities and exercises.)

The existing sales training program covers the basic sales process from opening to closing. There are practice activities on how to build rapport, ask questions, make presentations, handle objections, and listen. At the end of the workshop there is a final role play that puts all these skills together.

In the new version, we've created a self-study reading assignment from the content and overheads in this session. Our goal in the classroom session is to make sure that the student understands this information and then can apply it on the job. To meet this goal, we need to do two things. First, we have to develop a way to debrief and discuss the information in the self-study reading assignment. Second, we have to increase the practice activities from one big role play to several practice activities, so that we increase the participants' skill levels before they leave the class.

For our example, we are going to use "teach-backs" to discuss and debrief the content. In this activity, we divide the class into small teams. Each team is given a topic from the self-study reading assignment. Teams prepare brief presentations and then, in turn, make presentations to the class.

Several things happen with teach-backs that make them more effective than lectures. First, as a team prepares a presentation they are gaining additional insight and clarity as they discuss what they want to present. Second, the act of presenting information and trying to explain it to others quickly reveals what they do and do not know. Third, they hear information from others for a second or third time. This repetition helps increase retention.

The teach-backs are spaced out between practice activities. We would add enough practice so that everyone in the class has tried out and used every skill. This means that instead of one role play, we might do five or six. The coaches who lead the class are able to observe the leadership and communication skills of the students and the content knowledge that is demonstrated during the team activities. This input can help the coaches tailor their approach to the needs of different teams and individuals.

The leader's guide will make it easier for the facilitator/instructor, who is an experienced manager or supervisor, not a professional teacher or trainer. This guide will list the key points that should be made in each teach-back, so if the student doesn't make these points, the facilitator can add them.

The leader's guide will include other instructions for running the debriefing sessions and activities. The coaches do not have to teach the traditional way but are able to use their own experience and credibility to provide insight and advice to the students.

That's the mile-high view of how the classroom experience changes. Now we'll go into the details and give you some tips and techniques for making this approach really work.

Introductions

In a typical workshop, most of the first morning is lost to introductions, expectations, reviews of the agenda, and ground rules. For a one-day workshop, this doesn't leave a lot of time to accomplish anything.

Here are a number of ideas for streamlining the start of any seminar or workshop:

- Include the objectives and agenda for the session in the prework. Tell participants to review this material and send you their expectations for the session. Compile these expectations and then send them out an email to the class.

- Create or use your online bulletin board. Ask participants to post a brief bio or introduction to be read by other members of the class. This can include posting a digital picture.

- Bring participants together either the night before or right before the session in a structured, getting-acquainted activity.

- Hold a teleconference or videoconference a few days prior to the session to cover introduction basics.

- Build into the prework an activity that requires the participants to work with each other. This can include preparing a teach-back with another class member or posting the results of a research assignment on the online bulletin board.

Some of these pre-class activities help to reinforce the importance of the prework and provide an early warning about those who may not be prepared for the class. We find that some people even withdraw from the class at this point, while there is still enough time to move someone up from the waiting list.

Team Building

On their workshop evaluations, participants repeatedly say that working and learning from each other was the most valuable part of the class. Often, they are working on issues that are unrelated to the class. While you don't want to eliminate this interaction in class, you can structure it so that you can keep the session focused and on task. For example:

- Make sure that participants have each other's contact information so that they can keep in touch after the class.

- Create online bulletin boards and chat rooms so that participants will have a way to communicate before and after the class.

- Use a lot of small team activities in the class so that you promote discussion and interaction that is focused on the learning activities.

- Look at how the organization shares ideas when not in training. If you can improve that, it won't be the focus of the training session.

- Structure report-outs, sharing sessions, games, and hand-in assignments. These add a little pressure and a sense of competition that helps maintain focus and provides the coaches/instructors with plenty of opportunities to observe performance.

Practice Activities

Most of the classroom time will be transformed from lecture into practice. This means that you will be doing a lot of role plays and case studies. Here are a few design ideas for each.

Role Plays

Role plays should be used any time you are working on interactions with customers, team members, or employees. These would include sales calls, performance evaluations, interviews, conflict resolutions, and high-frequency calls from customers. It doesn't make much difference how you are going to do a role play if you are only doing one big role play. However, when we put the emphasis on practice we can easily do five or six role plays. If you can vary how role plays are done, you have a better chance of keeping everyone's attention. Here are a few ways you can try. We'll use a sales situation as an example:

Triads. Divide the class into threes. One person plays the customer, one person plays the salesperson, and the third acts as an observer, using a behavioral checklist. After the first role play, rotate roles until each person has had a chance to play all three parts.

Round Robin. The class sits in a semi-circle in front of the instructor. The instructor plays the role of the customer and the class plays the role of the salesperson. The person to the left of the instructor starts the role play. Each time the customer responds, the next participant picks up the call. This continues until the call is complete.

Tag Team. The class is divided into two teams, a customer team and a sales team. In front of the class there are two chairs, a customer chair and a salesperson chair. One person from each team sits in the chairs to start the role play. The rest of the class members stand behind their representatives. The two representatives start the role play. If either begins to have trouble, he or she can tag a team member, who will then sit in the chair and take over the call. Team members can also tag in at any time that they have something to add. Every team member must tag in at least once.

Presentation. The class is divided into small teams. Each team prepares a role play to present to the class. The team plays both roles. Each team then makes a presentation to the class and receives feedback.

One of the things that really slows down role plays is reading about each role. It's much easier if participants can see the customers or employees they are going to play. For this, we like to use short, digital videos. Let's assume we are going to be counseling six different employees about a performance problem. We script out and then produce a thirty-to-sixty-second video of the employee talking about the situation. (*You don't need professional actors for this.*)

We then embed all six videos into a PowerPoint slide. This allows us to click and play any video in any order at any time. One of the reasons we get great feedback on this approach is that it allows the participants to get a lot of nonverbal information that they would not find out from reading the role.

Case Studies

Case studies provide excellent practice for planning and problem-solving activities. They also require a lot of interaction between participants as well as giving them an opportunity to work on their presentation and writing skills. (*Just a quick aside:* Any time any activity teaches more than one skill at a time, this not only streamlines the training but also provides practice in combining skills as they are actually used.)

If you want to save time, there is no reason why participants can't read case-study materials before the class or at home between sessions. This also reduces the time some participants wait while others are still reading.

We do three things to improve case-study activities. First, we use short, digital videos to set up basic situations and introduce characters. Second, if we are going to use spreadsheets or other templates, we provide them on CD so that participants can work on them with their laptops during the session. Third, we have all presentations done in PowerPoint on a laptop. This has the rub-off effect of improving presentations skills and working with programs like PowerPoint and Excel. It also works very well to give participants templates in PowerPoint for their reports and presentations.

Real Situations

Instead of or in addition to case studies, we like to use real situations that participants bring to class. This can be an upcoming sales call, a workplace problem, or a planning activity. This type of practice activity is important because participants learn how to apply the concepts, content, and principles of the training to actual work situations.

It is always a challenge to transition learning from the classroom back to the job. We feel it helps to bring the job and the boss into the classroom. Many students tell us the class didn't feel like training. It felt like we were making progress on real work because the right people were there. They say it helped that a boss was available to provide tips and advice and to give the "go or no go" decisions when they needed it.

Often, just going from a case study to real life is not an easy transition.

Again, participants work on bringing in information for this activity prior to attending the class. We often ask them to send in a description of what they will be bringing about a week prior to the session.

Games

We like to use games as part of training sessions. One of the best uses of a game is to debrief or test knowledge that was included in the prework. You don't need to spend a lot of time creating games. A lot of prepackaged games can be projected onto a screen through your laptop. All you need to do is add the content. They are fun, interactive, and very professional.

Compliance

You've probably noticed that we ask participants to do a lot of work before coming to class. This has the advantage of allowing participants to work at their own speed and on their own time. It also creates a productive dialogue between participants, which will help them get the most out of the session.

The big question is how to get participants to actually do this work before a session. If prework is optional and it's acceptable to show up at a class without doing the work, you can be assured that only a small percentage of participants will have actually done the work.

First, there must be an organizational shift in thinking from the old way of doing training to the new way. Everyone in the organization must understand that this is how training will be done in the future and that they won't be able to participate in training unless they do the prework. This will only work, of course, if you have high-level support for training.

Second, you must put a tracking mechanism in place so you know who has done the work. This can include taking an online pre-test, sending in an action plan, sending in a list of expectations, or posting information on the class bulletin board. This all has to be done far enough in advance for the instructor to follow up with anyone who hasn't done the work.

Third, involve the participant's immediate supervisor or manager. If this person supports the training, the work will be done. Tell this supervisor or manager how much time the participant requires to do the prework and that you would like him or her to review and discuss this work with the participant prior to class. The manager should also have a similar role in review and debriefing after the class.

We find that it is important to send people home who come to class without having done the prework. It sends a powerful message about the way we are doing training. It also reinforces the people who did do the prework. Most importantly, you do not have to slow down to wait while the people who are not prepared catch up.

It's also very useful for supervisors and managers to have attended a class before sending others to it. This will ensure that they understand and support what's happening. Often, we invite the manager or supervisor to attend the first class with his or her employee. We like to involve managers in pilot programs to obtain their input. However, we don't want these managers in a passive observer role. When they attend they should always attend as participants so they experience the training first-hand.

Follow-Up

Finally, there must be a connection between classroom training and what happens on the job. In fact, the first few weeks after training will determine whether what was learned in the classroom will actually be used.

At the conclusion of every class, we add a follow-up activity. This is usually a report back to us on what happens on the job as the person tries to apply what he or she learned. For example, in a sales class they may have worked on an upcoming presentation with a real customer. We want them to report back to the class about what happened and how they used what was learned in the class.

We often use either a class email or a bulletin board to collect this information. Again, the participant's immediate supervisor or manager will be critical in making sure this follow-up is done. A simple tracking sheet with an email can work wonders. It has a list of participants, who sent the email, and those who have sent in their follow-up assignments.

In this chapter, we've described how the classroom experience changes when we move from lecture to practice activities. As you can see, the role of the instructor changes from that of being a presenter to being more of a facilitator and coach. This allows you to use managers as trainers rather than relying on professional trainers. This adds a lot of valuable, first-hand experience to the class.

Keep in mind that using Learning Paths as we have described them is a lot of change and that it will require you to look at all of the compliance and follow-up issues. But your bottom-line result will be more effective training that takes less time and costs less money.

Summary

More and more, a real premium is placed on classroom time. It's very expensive to bring employees into a classroom for long periods of time, especially when a lot of travel is involved. The key point we made in this chapter was that classrooms should be used for discussion and application rather than for the delivery of content. As we said, you can enable this process by making sure all the content is written down.

In the last several chapters, we have looked at how to make sure we are doing the training right. We've gone through all of the line items on a Learning Path and created new strategies for adding coaching, moved content to directed self-study, and revised the existing training classes.

A Final Note

IMAGINE AN ORGANIZATION where Learning Paths have become a way of life. Every function has a Learning Path that is measured and tied to business results. Most of the training has moved out of the classroom and into the field, shop floor, or office. Managers are leading the training effort as a way to be actively involved in coaching and developing their people. When there is a change in business direction, Learning Paths are quickly adjusted and retooled to reduce the chaos of change and to make sure the workforce is fully ready.

This is our vision of the role the training function should be playing within an organization. In this book, we've presented five major concepts that enable this vision to come to life.

Learning Paths Versus Curriculums

The first major shift was to begin to look at training as more than a series of courses loosely linked together. Instead, we wanted to look at everything that leads to proficiency and build it into a Learning Path that could easily be replicated for everyone, in particular, making sure that the amount of practice and experience required was captured and made part of the training.

Measuring Time Versus Training

Second, we recognized that there was a lot of value in measuring the time it took for employees to become proficient. All too often what was learned in the classroom or in self-study wasn't enough for employees to become proficient. By actually measuring Time to Proficiency we are able to see the possibilities for dramatically reducing the overall time of training while making it more effective.

In addition, by focusing on measuring Time to Proficiency we were able to provide a real measure of training that could be directly linked to business results. This level of objective measurement made it easier to justify expenditures on training.

Proficiency Versus Competency

Third, we could see that in almost every job it wasn't enough just to teach all the pieces and parts. Training had to focus on teaching how to use all the pieces and parts at the same time. It wasn't just learning the phone, the computer, and the sales pitch—it was being able to do all three things at the same time.

Managers Versus Trainers

Fourth, we felt that—with the addition of all the practice, experience, and self-study required in a Learning Path—that the training had to move out of the classroom and onto the job. This requires that managers become much more active in coaching and developing their people. However, one of the most important benefits of this change is that managers support and are better connected to the actual training.

Strategic Versus Tactical

Fifth, the Learning Paths Methodology enables the learning leader to take a more strategic role as the organization plans and implements change. We discussed at length how the role of the learning leader changes as Learning Paths become embedded in the organization. With this elevated role, there is even more support for Learning Paths.

As we worked on Learning Paths and began to see these five concepts in practice, it really had a significant effect on how we viewed training and the role of the learning leader within an organization. Much of the insight we gained you will start to experience as you lay out and measure your first Learning Path. There are always a lot of surprises at seeing it all on paper for the first time.

To start, we encourage you to try the 30/30 Plan, which has been laid out for you on the CD, where you will also find meeting invitations, meeting agendas, templates, and presentations that you can customize for your use. The most important part of making that plan work will be selecting a function that has a leader who will be a champion and real advocate for Learning Paths.

TO PUT THIS BOOK TOGETHER, we've worked with a number of business and training experts. As they reviewed the book for the first time, they asked a number of questions that they thought a reader might have. While you can find the answers to all of these questions in this book, we consolidated them here as a quick reference and summary for you.

1. Have you implemented Learning Paths anywhere or is this all just theory?

In its current form, we've implemented Learning Paths in a wide range of companies and industries over the past ten years. All of the examples in this book come directly from that experience. Since many of the examples come from consulting engagements where confidentiality agreements have been signed, we've refrained from mentioning any specific companies or people involved. In many cases, the immediate gains from Learning Paths come from a discipline and rigor that has seldom been applied on an enterprise-wide basis.

2. Isn't this just for larger companies with a lot of employees?

Most of the design and development of training happens in larger companies because of the resources available and the ability to spread the cost of training over a large number of employees. However, within these larger companies we've had great success in building Learning Paths for functions that have one or two employees. In environments with smaller numbers of employees, we tend to do less development of training and more selection of training that might already exist, such as a college course or an alternative approach like coaching or building job aids. The approach still works and may even be more important with a small and growing enterprise.

3. What if I don't have a lot of new employees?

We've focused this book and Learning Paths on new employees because it's clearer to see how to go from Day One to Proficiency. However, a Learning Path can also travel from a low level of performance to a high level of performance. And we've shown how having a Learning Path for everyone in the organization facilitates business planning. Even if there are a lot of new employees, building Learning Paths from Day One is often a good first step to building the path to high proficiency.

4. What's the difference between establishing a curriculum and a Learning Path?

As we discussed when we talked about how people really learn, going through a series of courses or a curriculum isn't enough to reach proficiency. There are a lot of other things that happen, including practice and live experience. Learning Paths try to capture everything that goes into learning something new and then puts a rigor and discipline around it.

5. How do you justify spending expensive manager time on training?

We think this is less an issue of expense and more an issue of priorities. One of the fastest and most effective ways managers can improve results in their areas of responsibility is to have employees who can do the job the manager wants at the level of performance the manager demands. This is very difficult to accomplish if the manager is not directly involved in the training and development of his or her subordinates. The reality is that many managers don't get involved in training either because they lack expertise in how an employee's job is done or they lack the expertise in training and coaching. That's why we try to add these pieces to a manager's Learning Path.

6. Can you really measure the impact of a Learning Path on bottom-line results?

Learning Paths are actually much easier to measure than traditional training is. Traditional training is difficult to measure because it's hard to isolate the effects of training from everything else that happens. With a Learning Path we are less concerned about the impact of any one given piece of training but rather on the overall Time to Proficiency. The simplest example of this is to look at the first day a salesperson makes a sale without any help. For example, if it's a new realtor, what was the first day he or she sold a house? If, before the Learning Path, the average first day was in six months and it was then reduced to three months, all of the sales from months three to six can be attributed to the Learning Path.

7. How do you actually get people to do all the self-study that replaces classroom training?

If you give someone a book to read and tell him or her to read it, it's unlikely that the book will get read. That's why when we talk about self-study we always mean *directed* self-study. This means that there are proscribed activities and interactions with a manager, trainer, or coach that ensure involvement. Here is an example of how directed self-study works.

> Manager: "At 2 p.m. today, you and I are going to go through a return vehicle inspection. Before we do that I want you to go through the "Inspections Self-Study." I will give you some time at 10 this morning. I expect you to be able to describe how we inspect vehicles and how to fill out the inspections report. If there is anything you don't understand in the Self-Study, make a list of questions and we'll go through them this afternoon."

8. What's the 30/30 Plan?

The 30/30 Plan stands for 30 percent reduction in a Learning Path in thirty days. This means that there is a new, revised Learning Path that is 30 percent faster that is now ready to implement. The reduction in time can't be fully verified until employees go through the new path and their Time to Proficiency is measured.

9. How can you get a reduction of 30 percent in a Learning Path so quickly?

There is really no secret. The first round of improvements comes from applying a rigor and discipline, including measurement, to a series of events that usually is very informal and not recorded. The reduction initially comes less from reducing the actual time spent in training than from reducing the time from the end of training until someone reaches proficiency. If you remember in the example about the assistant branch managers, where they weren't reaching proficiency for twelve to eighteen months, the improvement came from accelerating what was being done on a time-available basis only.

10. What's the difference between the 30/30 Plan and the full Learning Path Methodology?

There is always a lot of resistance to any change initiative. That's why getting early, measurable results is so important. We felt that, in the Learning Path Methodology, you could begin to implement a revised Learning Path after the Quick Hits step. The full methodology goes on to completely reengineer a Learning Path.

11. What resistance or obstacles can you expect when you try to implement Learning Paths?

The greatest barrier to implementing Learning Paths is that it is a change initiative. There is always a lot of individual and organizational resistance to change. To help with this change, we put in the 30/30 Plan to generate quick results and prove the methodology. However, there is never any substitute for high-level support and sponsorship.

12. Where do I start?

We recommend that you start with the 30/30 Plan. All of the details of that plan are on the CD that came with the book. It will take you through the basic steps of conducting a readiness assessment, selecting a function, and assembling a Learning Path Team.

THE LEARNING PATH TOOL KIT is a collection of the forms and templates presented in this book. The templates that you will need for the 30/30 Plan are also provided for you on the CD that came with this book. The templates included in this Tool Kit are

- Readiness Assessment
- Selecting a Function
- Selecting Learning Path Team Members
- Time to Proficiency Baseline Measures
- Time to Proficiency by New Employee
- Time to Proficiency Summary
- Learning Path Research Plan
- Learning Path Template

- Quick Hits Action Plan
- Learning Path Evaluation Checklist
- Proficiency Planning Process
- Learning Path Planning Process
- Learning Path Tracking Sheet
- Learning Path Project Plan
- Self-Study Project Plan
- Self-Study Tracking Sheet
- Cost Elements
- Training Method Comparison Sheet
- Transition Plan
- Transition Issues Action Plan

Readiness Assessment

Directions: *Rate each question from 1 to 5. 1 = Low and 5 = High. For any item rated as a 1, 2, or 3, write in a required action to address each issue.*

Questions	Rating	Required Actions
1. How important is reducing Time to Proficiency to your top management?	1 2 3 4 5	
2. How willing are your business leaders to be champions or sponsors for a Learning Path Initiative?	1 2 3 4 5	
3. How willing is the organization to commit the time of required individuals to actively participate on a Learning Path Team?	1 2 3 4 5	
4. How well do you understand the concepts and principles of the Learning Path Methodology?	1 2 3 4 5	
5. How well does your organization create and accept change?	1 2 3 4 5	
6. How willing are your current training staff, vendors, and consultants to participate in a Learning Path Initiative?	1 2 3 4 5	
7. What is the level of your organization's capability to conduct training research?	1 2 3 4 5	
8. What is the level of your organization's instructional design capabilities?	1 2 3 4 5	
9. What is the level of your organization's project management capabilities, including presentations and report writing?	1 2 3 4 5	
10. How willing are managers to coach and develop their people?	1 2 3 4 5	
11. How willing is the organization to commit financial resources if and when training needs to be updated, created, or revised?	1 2 3 4 5	
12. How well is formal on-the-job or self-study training accepted by the workforce.	1 2 3 4 5	
13. How willing is the workforce to share and discuss information about how they do their jobs?	1 2 3 4 5	
14. How experienced is your organization in measuring training and/or quality?	1 2 3 4 5	
15. How ready do you feel your organization is to begin a Learning Path Initiative?	1 2 3 4 5	

Selecting a Function

Function	# of Employees	Projected Growth	Management Support	Priority	Other Factors

Learning Paths. Copyright © 2004 by John Wiley & Sons, Inc. Reproduced by permission of Pfeiffer, an Imprint of Wiley. www.pfeiffer.com

Selecting Learning Path Team Members

Role	Description	Team Member
1. Executive Sponsor or Champion	- Ensure that resources and time are allocated to this initiative - Address any organizational issues or barriers	
2. Project Leader	- Conduct team meetings - Manage the logistics and communications of the initiative - Train team members in the Learning Path Methodology	
3. Subject-Matter Expert	- Ensure that the content covered in the Learning Path is current and complete - Ensure that the research is accurate and complete	
4. Training Leader	- Making sure that the training resources are available and funded to implement this initiative.	
5. Instructional Designer	- Ensure that any changes to the Learning Path are instructionally sound - Provide insight into how to improve the Learning Path	
6. Quality Leader	- Provide expertise in measuring training and business results	
7. Other Stakeholders	- Provide experience and validation on how selected functions are performed and measured	

Learning Paths. Copyright © 2004 by John Wiley & Sons, Inc. Reproduced by permission of Pfeiffer, an Imprint of Wiley. www.pfeiffer.com

Time to Proficiency Baseline Measures

Performance Measure	How It's Measured	Average Performance	High Performance

Time to Proficiency by New Employee

Employee	Date of Hire	Classroom Days	Coaching Days	Days to Proficiency
Total/Average				

Time to Proficiency Summary

Number of Employees by Class	Classroom Days	Coaching Days	Days to Proficiency
Total/Average			

Learning Path Research Plan

Job or Function: _____   Today's Date: _____   Estimated Completion Date: _____

Research Activity	Action Steps (Who, What, Where, and How)	Conducted by	When

Learning Path Template

Function: _____   **Date:** _____

Day	What	How	Materials	Done

Quick Hits Action Plan

Job or Function: _____ Today's Date: _____ Estimated Completion Date: _____

Quick Hits	How	Who	When

Learning Path Evaluation Checklist

Factor	Rating	Required Actions
1. Information, policies, and procedures are current, complete, and correct.	1 2 3 4 5	
2. Content has been moved from classroom delivery to self-study.	1 2 3 4 5	
3. Managers have assumed the role of coaches and direct all self-study.	1 2 3 4 5	
4. The Learning Path is sequenced around tasks, functions, and processes rather than topics.	1 2 3 4 5	
5. Tasks, functions, and processes are sequenced from simple to complex.	1 2 3 4 5	
6. Test and measurements are used to track progress along the Learning Path.	1 2 3 4 5	
7. The gap between Graduation and Independence Day has been closed.	1 2 3 4 5	
8. Practice and experience has been quantified and included in the Learning Path.	1 2 3 4 5	
9. Each line item has been evaluated to make sure it is the most appropriate way to deliver that training.	1 2 3 4 5	
10. Strategies are in place to keep employees motivated in engaged.	1 2 3 4 5	

Proficiency Planning Process

Business Objective #1:		
Proposed Actions	**Changes to Jobs or Functions**	**Change to Proficiencies**
1.		
2.		
3.		

Learning Paths. Copyright © 2004 by John Wiley & Sons, Inc. Reproduced by permission of Pfeiffer, an Imprint of Wiley. www.pfeiffer.com

Learning Path Planning Process

Change to Proficiency	Changes to Learning Path	Timeline	Cost
1.			
2.			
3.			

Learning Paths. Copyright © 2004 by John Wiley & Sons, Inc. Reproduced by permission of Pfeiffer, an Imprint of Wiley. www.pfeiffer.com

Learning Path Tracking Sheet

Job or Function: _____ **Today's Date:** _____ **Estimated Completion Date:** _____

Steps	How	Who	Due	Done
1. Identify and recruit team members				
2. Hold team kickoff planning meeting				
3. Develop research plan				
4. Conduct research				
5. Develop and present research report				
6. Map current Learning Path				
7. Gather baseline data				
8. Identify Quick Hits				
9. Create plan for implementing Quick Hits				
10. Build a proficiency model				
11. Align proficiency model to business needs				
12. Determine how to accelerate the Learning Path				
13. Build required training				
14. Revise Learning Path with new training				
15. Measure results				
16. Create maintenance plan				

Red = Alert needs immediate attention   Yellow = Delayed or Behind Schedule   Green = On Track

Learning Path Project Plan

Functions	Select Team Members	Kickoff	Define Time to Proficiency	Map Learning Path	Quick Hits	Acceleration	New Learning Path	Transition	Maintenance	Comments

Red = Alert needs immediate attention   Yellow = Delayed or Behind Schedule   Green = On Track

Learning Paths. Copyright © 2004 by John Wiley & Sons, Inc. Reproduced by permission of Pfeiffer, an Imprint of Wiley. www.pfeiffer.com

Self-Study Project Plan

Job or Function: _____ Today's Date: _____ Estimated Completion Date: _____

Course	Outline	Review	Research	Review	First Draft	Review	Revisions	Review	Edit and Proof	Production	Comments

Red = Alert needs immediate attention Yellow = Delayed or behind schedule Green = On track

Self-Study Tracking Sheet

Function	# of Course	Outline	Research	First Draft	Revisions	Edit and Proof	Production	Comments

Red = Alert needs immediate attention Yellow = Delayed or behind schedule Green = On track

Cost Elements

	Classroom	On the Job	One-on-One Tutorial	Practice	Coaching	Simulations	New Learning Path	Synchronous Self-Study eLearning	Asynchronous Self-Study Text Online
Staff Salaries									
Planners/Leaders									
Developers									
Instructors									
Subject-Matter Experts									
Students									
Programs									
Tuition/Fees									
Materials									
Maintenance/ Updates									
Contract Developers									
Contract Instructors									
Travel									
Planners									
Developers									
Instructors									
Subject-Matter Experts									
Students									
Facilities									
Offices									
Classrooms									
On the Job									
Equipment									
Systems LMS									
Learning Mgmt System									
Office Supplies									

Training Method Comparison Sheet

Method	Effectiveness	Cost	Speed	Flexibility	Barriers
Job Aids					
Training Meetings					
Self-Study Reading					
eLearning					
Video					
Audio					
Classroom					

Transition Plan

Job or Function: _____   Today's Date: _____   Estimated Completion Date: _____

	Jan.	Feb.	March	April	May	June	July	Aug.	Sept.	Oct.	Nov.	Dec.
Phase 1: Measurement												
Phase 2: Map Out Current Learning Path												
Phase 3: Quick Hits												
Phase 4: Build New Training												
Phase 5: Roll-Out												

Transition Issues Action Plan

Job or Function: _____ Today's Date: _____ Estimated Completion Date: _____

Issues	Actions	Who	When

WORKING ON LEARNING PATHS and with a Learning Path Team often requires a wide range of expertise and experience. The following lists of books, websites, and newsletters may provide additional insights, ideas, strategies, and techniques.

Change Management

Birnbaum, W.S. (1990). *If your strategy is so terrific how come it doesn't work?* New York: AMACOM.

Brill, P.L., & Worth, R. (1997). *The four levers of corporate change.* New York: AMACOM.

Change Management Resource Library. Books, articles, training, websites, and consultants. Available: www.change-management.org.

Chawla, S., & Renesch, J. (1995). *Learning organizations: Developing cultures for tomorrow's workplace.* Portland, OR: Productivity Press.

Collins, J.C., & Porras, J.I. (1994). *Built to last.* New York: HarperCollins.

Conner, D.R. (1992). *Managing at the speed of change: How resilient managers succeed and prosper where others fail.* New York: Villard Books.

O'Boyle, T.F. (1998). *At any cost: Jack Welch, General Electric, and the pursuit of profit.* New York: Vintage Books.

Reichheld, F.F. (1996). *The loyalty effect: The hidden force behind profits and lasting value.* Boston, MA: HBS Press.

Schein, E. (1965). *Organizational psychology.* Upper Saddle River, NJ: Prentice-Hall.

Senge, P.M. (1990). *The fifth discipline: The art & practice of the learning organization.* New York: Currency/Doubleday.

Slater, R. (2000). *The GE way fieldbook: Jack Welch's battle plan for corporate revolution.* New York: McGraw-Hill.

Coaching

Armour, T. (1953). *How to play your best golf all the time.* New York: Simon & Schuster.

Bell, C.R. (2002). *Managers as mentor: Building partnerships for learning.* San Francisco, CA: Berrett-Koehler.

International Coach Federation. Non-profit professional association of personal and business coaches with resources and training for coaches and referral service. Available: www.coachfederation.org.

Smart, B.D. (1999). *Top grading: How leading companies win by hiring, coaching, and keeping the best people.* Upper Saddle River, NJ: Prentice-Hall.

Call Center Newsletter. Available at: www.callcenterops.com/newsletter.htm.

Consulting

Block, P. (2000). *Flawless consulting* (2nd ed.). San Francisco, CA: Pfeiffer.

Juran, J.M. (1964). *Managerial breakthrough: A new concept of the manager's job.* New York: McGraw-Hill.

Kouzes, J.M., & Posner, B.Z. (1987). *The leadership challenge: How to get extraordinary things done in organizations.* San Francisco, CA: Jossey-Bass.

Schein, E. (1969). *Process consultation: It's role in organization development.* Reading, MA: Addison-Wesley.

Schwarz, R.M. (1994). *The skilled facilitator: Practical wisdom for developing effective groups.* San Francisco, CA: Jossey-Bass.

Scott, B. (2000). *Consulting on the inside.* Alexandria, VA: ASTD Press.

Slater, R. (1999). *Jack Welch and the GE way: Management insights and leadership secrets of the legendary CEO.* New York: McGraw-Hill.

Steele, F. (1982). *The role of the internal consultant.* Boston, MA: CBI Publishing.

e-Learning

Driscoll, M. (1998). *Web-based training: Using technology to design adult learning experiences.* San Francisco, CA: Pfeiffer.

Kruse, K., & Keil, J. (2000). *Technology-based training: The art and science of design, development, and delivery.* San Francisco, CA: Pfeiffer.

Rosenberg, M.J. (2001). *e-Learning: Strategies for delivering knowledge in the digital age.* New York: McGraw-Hill.

Schank, R.C. (2002). *Designing world-class e-learning: How IBM, GE, Harvard Business School, and Columbia University are succeeding at e-learning.* New York: McGraw-Hill.

Knowledge Management

CIO Magazine. Knowledge Management resources, including selecting and organizing the intellectual capital of a company. Available: www.cio.com.

Clemmon-Rumizen, M. (2001). *The complete idiot's guide to knowledge management.* East Rutherford, NJ: Alpha Books.

Drucker, P.F. (1998). *Harvard Business Review on knowledge management* (Harvard Business Review Series). Boston, MA: Harvard Business School Press.

Hartley, D.E. (2000). *On-demand learning: Training in the new millennium.* Amherst, MA: HRD Press.

Knowledge Management Resource Center. Knowledge management sites, periodicals, news, forums, articles, supported by IDG Corporation. Available: www.cio.com.

Leadership

Bennis, W., & Nanus, B. (1985). *Leaders: The strategies for taking charge.* New York: Harper & Row.

Center for Creative Leadership. International, nonprofit educational institution that focuses on developing models of managerial practice. Available: www.ccl.org.

Hersey, P. (1984). *The situational leader.* New York: Warner Books.

Learning Theory

American Society for Training and Development. Training and development tools, conferences, books, and articles. Available: www.astd.org.

Albrecht, K. (1980). *Brain power.* Englewood Cliffs, NJ: Prentice-Hall.

Bloom, B.S. (1976). *Human characteristics and school learning.* New York: McGraw-Hill.

Bloom, B.S. (1956). *Taxonomy of educational objectives.* New York: David McKay.

Knowles, M.S. (1973). *The adult learner: A neglected species.* Burlington, MA: Gulf Professional Publishing.

Knowles, M.S. (1970). *The modern practice of adult education.* Chicago: Association Press.

Mager, R.F. (1997). *The new Mager six-pack.* Atlanta, GA: CEP Press.

Revans, R.W. (1980). *Action learning: New techniques for management.* London: Blond & Briggs.

Rogers, C.R. (1969). *Freedom to learn.* Columbus, OH: Charles E. Merrill.

Senge, P. (1994). *The fifth discipline fieldbook.* New York: Doubleday.

Training Magazine. A resource for training professionals with information on research, materials, education, and employment. Available: www. trainingmag.com.

Performance Management

Buckingham, M., & Coffman, C. (1999). *First, break all the rules: What the world's greatest managers do differently.* New York: Simon & Schuster.

Covey, S.R. (1989). *The seven habits of highly effective people: Restoring the character ethic.* New York: Simon & Schuster.

Dixon, G. (1988). *What works at work: Lessons from the masters: Personal profiles of 27 workplace experts and the 10 most important lessons they've learned about people, performance, and productivity.* Minneapolis, MN: Lakewood Books.

Goleman, D. (1995). *Emotional intelligence: Why it can matter more than IQ.* New York: Bantam Books.

Goleman, D. (1998). *Working with emotional intelligence.* Los Angeles: Audio Renaissance.

Hersey, P., & Blanchard, K.H. (1982). *Management of organization behavior: Utilizing human resources.* Upper Saddle River, NJ: Prentice-Hall.

International Society for Performance Improvement. Resources for improving productivity and performance in the workplace through human performance technology. Available: www.ispi.org.

Meier, D. (2000). *The accelerated learning handbook: A creative guide to designing and delivering faster, more effective training programs.* New York: McGraw-Hill.

Phillips, J.J., & Stone, R.D. (2002). *How to measure training results: A practical guide to tracking the six key indicators.* New York: McGraw-Hill.

Society for Human Resource Management. Human resource management tools, conferences, certification, books, and articles. Available: www.shrm.org.

Workforce Week Newsletter: Available: www.callcenterops.com/newsletter.htm.

Project Management

The Project Management Institute. Nonprofit professional association in the area of project management. Available: www.pmi.org.

Decision Making and Facilitation Tools. Available: www.mindtools.com.

Verzuh, E. (1999). *The fast forward MBA in project management: Quick tips, speedy solutions, and cutting-edge ideas.* New York: John Wiley & Sons.

Bruce, A., & Langdon, K. (2000). *Essential managers: Project management* (Essential Managers Series). New York: DK Publishing.

Problem Solving

Adams, J.L. (1974). *Conceptual block-busting: A pleasurable guide to better problem solving.* New York: W. W. Norton.

Fisher, R. & Ury, W. (1981). *Getting to yes.* Boston, MA: Houghton Mifflin.

Hodnett, E. (1955). *The art of problem solving: How to improve your methods.* New York: Harper & Row.

Jackson, K.F. (1975). *The art of solving problems.* New York: St. Martin's Press.

Karrass, C.L. (1987). *Effective negotiating.* Santa Monica, CA: Karrass Seminars.

Osborn, A.F. (1963). *Applied imagination: Principles and procedures of creative problem solving* (3rd ed.). New York: Charles Scribner's Sons.

Prince, G.M. (1970). *The practice of creativity: A manual for dynamic group problem solving.* New York: Collier.

Quality

American Society for Quality. Quality tools, conferences, certification, books, and articles. Available: www.asq.org.

DeFeo, J.A., & Barnard, W.W. (2003). *Juran Institute's six sigma breakthrough and beyond: Quality performance breakthrough methods.* New York: McGraw-Hill.

Grant, E.L., & Leavenworth, R.S. (1980). *Statistical quality control* (5th ed.). New York: McGraw-Hill.

Gupta, P. (2003). *Six sigma business scorecard: Creating a comprehensive corporate performance measurement system.* New York: McGraw-Hill.

Juran, J.M. (1989). *Juran on leadership for quality: An executive handbook.* New York: The Free Press.

Juran, J. M. (1988). *Juran on planning for quality.* New York: The Free Press.

Pyzdek, T. (2003). *The six sigma project planner: A step-by-step guide to leading a six sigma project through DMAIC.* New York: McGraw-Hill.

Team Building

Katzenbach, J.R., & Smith, D.K. (1993). *The wisdom of teams.* Boston, MA: Harvard Business School Press.

Pfeiffer, J.W. (Ed.). (1991). *The encyclopedia of team-building activities.* San Francisco, CA: Pfeiffer.

Pfeiffer, J.W. (Ed.). (1991). *The encyclopedia of team-development activities.* San Francisco, CA: Pfeiffer.

Scholtes, P.E., Joiner, B.L., & Streibel, B.J. (1996). *The team handbook* (2nd ed.). Madison, WI: Joiner Associates.

INDEX

S TEVE ROSENBAUM AND JIM WILLIAMS began working together in 1996 when Jim joined GE to lead the training function for one of the GE Capital businesses. Steve worked with Jim, along with many other clients, as an external consultant, instructional designer, and writer. Out of this collaboration, the concept of Learning Paths was developed, implemented, tested, and proven.

Jim Williams is a training and development leader with over twenty years' experience creating and implementing training solutions to support organizational change and growth initiatives, first at IBM and then at GE. At GE Jim was the Chief Learning Officer for Business Process Outsourcing work in India and set up the learning function for GE's outsourcing in Eastern Europe in Budapest, Hungary. He developed award-winning sales training at GE Capital and used a blended approach of online and classroom learning to help change the way salespeople go to market and the way sales leaders coach. At IBM Jim held various leadership roles in training functions, including leadership development, quality improvement, and pioneering the use of distance learning for technical vitality.

Over the past twenty-three years, Steve Rosenbaum has worked with America's leading companies, including Disney, DuPont, GE Capital, Ceridian, IBM, and Carlson Companies, to help them design, develop, and implement creative training solutions. He has worked both as an independent consultant and as a subcontractor to larger training and consulting firms. Steve has extensive experience designing and developing training for call centers, sales forces, customer service agents, managers, and internal consultants. He has worked in almost every industry from banking to high tech to health care to manufacturing. Steve has developed training and led training projects in a wide range of delivery methods. Steve has also written two other books, *Managing and Measuring Productivity* and *Fair Employment Interviewing*. Steve brings to the book a broad business prospective from the outside looking in.

System Requirements

PC with Microsoft Windows 98SE or later

Mac with Apple OS version 8.6 or later

Using the CD with Windows

To view the items located on the CD, follow these steps:

1. Insert the CD into your computer's CD-ROM drive.

2. A window appears with the following options:

   Contents: Allows you to view the files included on the CD-ROM.

   Software: Allows you to install useful software from the CD-ROM.

   Links: Displays a hyperlinked page of websites.

   Author: Displays a page with information about the author(s).

Contact Us: Displays a page with information on contacting the publisher or author.

Help: Displays a page with information on using the CD.

Exit: Closes the interface window.

If you do not have autorun enabled, or if the autorun window does not appear, follow these steps to access the CD:

1. Click Start -> Run.

2. In the dialog box that appears, type d:<\\>start.exe, where d is the letter of your CD-ROM drive. This brings up the autorun window described in the preceding set of steps.

3. Choose the desired option from the menu. (See Step 2 in the preceding list for a description of these options.)

In Case of Trouble

If you experience difficulty using the CD-ROM, please follow these steps:

1. Make sure your hardware and systems configurations conform to the systems requirements noted under "System Requirements" above.

2. Review the installation procedure for your type of hardware and operating system.

It is possible to reinstall the software if necessary.

To speak with someone in Product Technical Support, call 800–762–2974 or 317–572–3994 M–F 8:30 a.m. – 5:00 p.m. EST. You can also get support and contact Product Technical Support through our website at www.wiley.com/techsupport.

Before calling or writing, please have the following information available:

- Type of computer and operating system
- Any error messages displayed
- Complete description of the problem.

It is best if you are sitting at your computer when making the call.

Pfeiffer Publications Guide

This guide is designed to familiarize you with the various types of Pfeiffer publications. The formats section describes the various types of products that we publish; the methodologies section describes the many different ways that content might be provided within a product. We also provide a list of the topic areas in which we publish.

FORMATS

In addition to its extensive book-publishing program, Pfeiffer offers content in an array of formats, from fieldbooks for the practitioner to complete, ready-to-use training packages that support group learning.

FIELDBOOK Designed to provide information and guidance to practitioners in the midst of action. Most fieldbooks are companions to another, sometimes earlier, work, from which its ideas are derived; the fieldbook makes practical what was theoretical in the original text. Fieldbooks can certainly be read from cover to cover. More likely, though, you'll find yourself bouncing around following a particular theme, or dipping in as the mood, and the situation, dictate.

HANDBOOK A contributed volume of work on a single topic, comprising an eclectic mix of ideas, case studies, and best practices sourced by practitioners and experts in the field.

An editor or team of editors usually is appointed to seek out contributors and to evaluate content for relevance to the topic. Think of a handbook not as a ready-to-eat meal, but as a cookbook of ingredients that enables you to create the most fitting experience for the occasion.

RESOURCE Materials designed to support group learning. They come in many forms: a complete, ready-to-use exercise (such as a game); a comprehensive resource on one topic (such as conflict management) containing a variety of methods and approaches; or a collection of like-minded activities (such as icebreakers) on multiple subjects and situations.

TRAINING PACKAGE An entire, ready-to-use learning program that focuses on a particular topic or skill. All packages comprise a guide for the facilitator/trainer and a workbook for the participants. Some packages are supported with additional media—such as video—or learning aids, instruments, or other devices to help participants understand concepts or practice and develop skills.

- *Facilitator/trainer's guide* Contains an introduction to the program, advice on how to organize and facilitate the learning event, and step-by-step instructor notes. The guide also contains copies of presentation materials—handouts, presentations, and overhead designs, for example—used in the program.

- *Participant's workbook* Contains exercises and reading materials that support the learning goal and serves as a valuable reference and support guide for participants in the weeks and months that follow the learning event. Typically, each participant will require his or her own workbook.

ELECTRONIC CD-ROMs and web-based products transform static Pfeiffer content into dynamic, interactive experiences. Designed to take advantage of the searchability, automation, and ease-of-use that technology provides, our e-products bring convenience and immediate accessibility to your workspace.

METHODOLOGIES

CASE STUDY A presentation, in narrative form, of an actual event that has occurred inside an organization. Case studies are not prescriptive, nor are they used to prove a point; they are designed to develop critical analysis and decision-making skills. A case study has a specific time frame, specifies a sequence of events, is narrative in structure, and contains a plot structure— an issue (what should be/have been done?). Use case studies when the goal is to enable participants to apply previously learned theories to the circumstances in the case, decide what is pertinent, identify the real issues, decide what should have been done, and develop a plan of action.

ENERGIZER A short activity that develops readiness for the next session or learning event. Energizers are most commonly used after a break or lunch to stimulate or refocus the group. Many involve some form of physical activity, so they are a useful way to counter post-lunch lethargy. Other uses include transitioning from one topic to another, where "mental" distancing is important.

EXPERIENTIAL LEARNING ACTIVITY (ELA) A facilitator-led intervention that moves participants through the learning cycle from experience to application (also known as a Structured Experience). ELAs are carefully thought-out designs in which there is a definite learning purpose and intended outcome. Each step—everything that participants do during the activity— facilitates the accomplishment of the stated goal. Each ELA includes complete instructions for facilitating the intervention and a clear statement of goals, suggested group size and timing, materials required, an explanation of the process, and, where appropriate, possible variations to the activity. (For more detail on Experiential Learning Activities, see the Introduction to the *Reference Guide to Handbooks and Annuals*, 1999 edition, Pfeiffer, San Francisco.)

GAME A group activity that has the purpose of fostering team spirit and togetherness in addition to the achievement of a pre-stated goal. Usually contrived—undertaking a desert expedition, for example—this type of learning method offers an engaging means for participants to demonstrate and practice business and interpersonal skills. Games are effective for team building and personal development mainly because the goal is subordinate to the process—the means through which participants reach decisions, collaborate, communicate, and generate trust and understanding. Games often engage teams in "friendly" competition.

ICEBREAKER A (usually) short activity designed to help participants overcome initial anxiety in a training session and/or to acquaint the participants with one another. An icebreaker can be a fun activity or can be tied to specific topics or training goals. While a useful tool in itself, the icebreaker comes into its own in situations where tension or resistance exists within a group.

INSTRUMENT A device used to assess, appraise, evaluate, describe, classify, and summarize various aspects of human behavior. The term used to describe an instrument depends primarily on its format and purpose. These terms include survey, questionnaire, inventory, diagnostic, survey, and poll. Some uses of instruments include providing instrumental feedback to group members, studying here-and-now processes or functioning within a group, manipulating group composition, and evaluating outcomes of training and other interventions.

Instruments are popular in the training and HR field because, in general, more growth can occur if an individual is provided with a method for focusing specifically on his or her own behavior. Instruments also are used to obtain information that will serve as a basis for change and to assist in workforce planning efforts.

Paper-and-pencil tests still dominate the instrument landscape with a typical package comprising a facilitator's guide, which offers advice on administering the instrument and interpreting the collected data, and an initial set of instruments. Additional instruments are available separately. Pfeiffer, though, is investing heavily in e-instruments. Electronic instrumentation provides effortless distribution and, for larger groups particularly, offers advantages over paper-and-pencil tests in the time it takes to analyze data and provide feedback.

LECTURETTE A short talk that provides an explanation of a principle, model, or process that is pertinent to the participants' current learning needs. A lecturette is intended to establish a common language bond between the trainer and the participants by providing a mutual frame of reference. Use a lecturette as an introduction to a group activity or event, as an interjection during an event, or as a handout.

MODEL A graphic depiction of a system or process and the relationship among its elements. Models provide a frame of reference and something more tangible, and more easily remembered, than a verbal explanation. They also give participants something to "go on," enabling them to track their own progress as they experience the dynamics, processes, and relationships being depicted in the model.

ROLE PLAY A technique in which people assume a role in a situation/scenario: a customer service rep in an angry-customer exchange, for example. The way in which the role is approached is then discussed and feedback is offered. The role play is often repeated using a different approach and/or incorporating changes made based on feedback received. In other words, role playing is a spontaneous interaction involving realistic behavior under artificial (and safe) conditions.

SIMULATION A methodology for understanding the interrelationships among components of a system or process. Simulations differ from games in that they test or use a model that depicts or mirrors some aspect of reality in form, if not necessarily in content. Learning occurs by studying the effects of change on one or more factors of the model. Simulations are commonly used to test hypotheses about what happens in a system—often referred to as "what if?" analysis—or to examine best-case/worst-case scenarios.

THEORY A presentation of an idea from a conjectural perspective. Theories are useful because they encourage us to examine behavior and phenomena through a different lens.

TOPICS

The twin goals of providing effective and practical solutions for workforce training and organization development and meeting the educational needs of training and human resource professionals shape Pfeiffer's publishing program. Core topics include the following:

Leadership & Management

Communication & Presentation

Coaching & Mentoring

Training & Development

E-Learning

Teams & Collaboration

OD & Strategic Planning

Human Resources

Consulting

What will you find on pfeiffer.com?

- The best in workplace performance solutions for training and HR professionals

- Downloadable training tools, exercises, and content

- Web-exclusive offers

- Training tips, articles, and news

- Seamless on-line ordering

- Author guidelines, information on becoming a Pfeiffer Affiliate, and much more

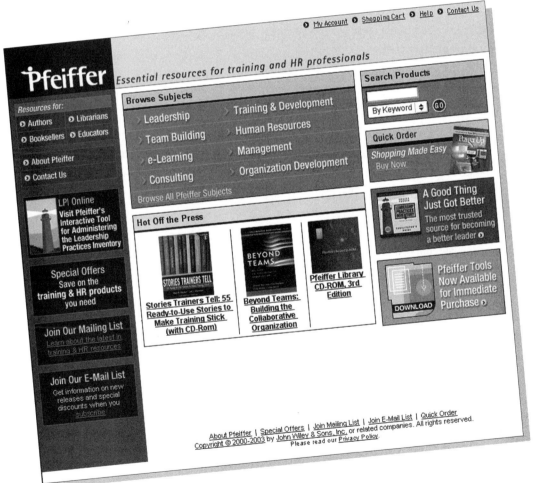

Discover more at www.pfeiffer.com

Customer Care

Have a question, comment, or suggestion? Contact us! We value your feedback and we want to hear from you.

For questions about this or other Pfeiffer products, you may contact us by:

E-mail: **customer@wiley.com**

Mail: **Customer Care Wiley/Pfeiffer**
        10475 Crosspoint Blvd.
        Indianapolis, IN 46256

Phone: **(US) 800-274-4434** (Outside the US: 317-572-3985)

Fax: **(US) 800-569-0443** (Outside the US: 317-572-4002)

To order additional copies of this title or to browse other Pfeiffer products, visit us online at **www.pfeiffer.com**.

For **Technical Support** questions call **(800) 274-4434**.

For authors guidelines, log on to www.pfeiffer.com and click on "Resources for Authors."

If you are . . .

A **college bookstore, a professor, an instructor, or work in higher education** and you'd like to place an order or request an exam copy, please contact jbreview@wiley.com.

A **general retail bookseller** and you'd like to establish an account or speak to a local sales representative, contact Melissa Grecco at 201-748-6267 or mgrecco@wiley.com.

An **exclusively on-line bookseller**, contact Amy Blanchard at 530-756-9456 or ablanchard@wiley.com or Jennifer Johnson at 206-568-3883 or jjohnson@wiley.com, both of our Online Sales department.

A **librarian or library representative**, contact John Chambers in our Library Sales department at 201-748-6291 or jchamber@wiley.com.

A **reseller, training company/consultant, or corporate trainer**, contact Charles Regan in our Special Sales department at 201-748-6553 or cregan@wiley.com.

A **specialty retail distributor** (includes specialty gift stores, museum shops, and corporate bulk sales), contact Kim Hendrickson in our Special Sales department at 201-748-6037 or khendric@wiley.com.

Purchasing for the **Federal government**, contact Ron Cunningham in our Special Sales department at 317-572-3053 or rcunning@wiley.com.

Purchasing for a **State or Local government**, contact Charles Regan in our Special Sales department at 201-748-6553 or cregan@wiley.com.